Understanding The Holy Temple of the Old Testament

From the Tabernacle to Solomon's Temple & Beyond

LEEN & KATHLEEN RITMEYER

cartaJerusalem

First published in 2016 by
CARTA Jerusalem

Sections of this book have appeared previously in other titles authored by
Leen & Kathleen Ritmeyer and published by Carta.

11 Rivka Street, P.O.B. 2500,
Jerusalem 9102401, Israel
E-mail: carta@carta.co.il
www.carta-jerusalem.com

ISBN: 978-965-220-881-1

Printed in the United States of America

CONTENTS

INTRODUCTION

Principles of Holiness

In the Hebrew Bible, the Temple of Jerusalem is referred to as the Holy Temple, e.g., in the Book of Psalms 5:7; 11:4; 65:4; 79:1 and 138:2, and elsewhere. The Holy Temple in Jerusalem was a building designed to house the Ark of the Covenant and to serve as a central place to worship the God of Israel. But why is it called Holy and what does this mean? The word "holy" means to be separate or set apart.

Isaiah the prophet wrote that the LORD resides in heaven:

> *Thus saith the LORD, the heaven is my throne, and the earth is my footstool: where is the house that ye build unto me? and where is the place of my rest? For all those things hath mine hand made, and those things have been, saith the LORD: but to this man will I look, even to him that is poor and of a contrite spirit, and trembleth at my word.* (Isa. 66:1,2)

But David said in the Book of Psalms (11:4):

> *The LORD is in his Holy Temple, the LORD's throne is in heaven: his eyes behold, his eyelids try, the children of men.*

God therefore dwells in the heavens, but His presence is also in the Temple, from where He observes the heart of men. The Temple was set apart from all other buildings as a house for the Deity. That is the reason why the Temple is called the Holy Temple. Entrance to the Temple was restricted to priests only, with the inner sanctuary accessible only to the High Priest once a year. Solomon was the first king to build a temple on Mount Moriah, but the worship of God and the sanctity of the Israelite sanctuary began much earlier in history.

(overleaf) Michelangelo's The Creation of Man. *Detail, ceiling of Sistine Chapel, Vatican.*

THE GENESIS SANCTUARY

In the early chapters of Genesis we read that God created a garden in Eden and placed Adam and Eve in it to look after it. God Himself walked in this garden (Gen. 3:8) and therefore it represented the dwelling place of God, comparable to the Holy of Holies of the later Tabernacle and Jerusalem Temples. God spoke in the Garden of Eden and also in the Holy of Holies that is sometimes called *debir* (oracle, derived from *dabar*, to speak). A similar expression of God walking in a sacred space is used of the Tabernacle:

> *And I will set my tabernacle among you: and my soul shall not abhor you.*
> *And I will walk among you, and will be your God, and ye shall be my people.* (Lev. 26:11,12)

One of the earliest extra-biblical references to the Garden of Eden being a representation of the Temple comes from the apocryphal Book of Jubilees 8:19: *"[Noah] knew that the Garden of Eden is the holy of holies, and the dwelling place of the Lord."*

Adam was given a charge to dress (*abad*—work) and keep (*shamar*—watch) the garden:

> *And the LORD God took the man, and put him into the Garden of Eden to dress it and to keep it.* (Gen. 2:15)

The Hebrew verbs 'to dress' and 'to keep' are also used to describe the work of the priests in the Tabernacle:

> *Bring the tribe of Levi near, and present them before Aaron the priest, that they may minister unto him. And they shall keep his charge (derived from* shamar*), and the charge of the whole congregation before the tabernacle of the congregation, to do the service (derived from* abad*) of the tabernacle.* (Num. 3:6,7)

It could be suggested therefore that Adam was given a priestly duty to look after this garden-sanctuary[1]. After Adam and Eve had transgressed God's commandment forbidding them to eat of the Tree of the Knowledge of Good and Evil, the LORD God said:

> *Behold, the man is become as one of us, to know good and evil: and now, lest he put forth his hand, and take also of the tree of life, and eat, and live for ever: Therefore the LORD God sent him forth from the garden of Eden, to till the ground from whence he was taken. So he drove out the man; and he placed at the east of the Garden of Eden Cherubim, and a flaming sword which turned every way, to keep the way of the tree of life.* (Gen. 3:22–24)

The Proto-Tabernacle

Adam and Eve were now exiled from the Garden of Eden. To prevent their return, cherubim with a flaming sword that turned in all directions, were placed to the east of the garden. In Hebrew, the word "placed" (*yasken*), in Genesis 3:24, is related to the word for Tabernacle, which is *mishkan*. The original language appears to indicate that the cherubim were made to dwell in a tent-sanctuary or tabernacle that was erected to the east of the Garden of Eden[2]. Although little else is known about this sanctuary, the text would seem to be describing a proto-Tabernacle, which would serve as a model for future meeting places between God and man **(Fig. 1)**.

Fig. 1

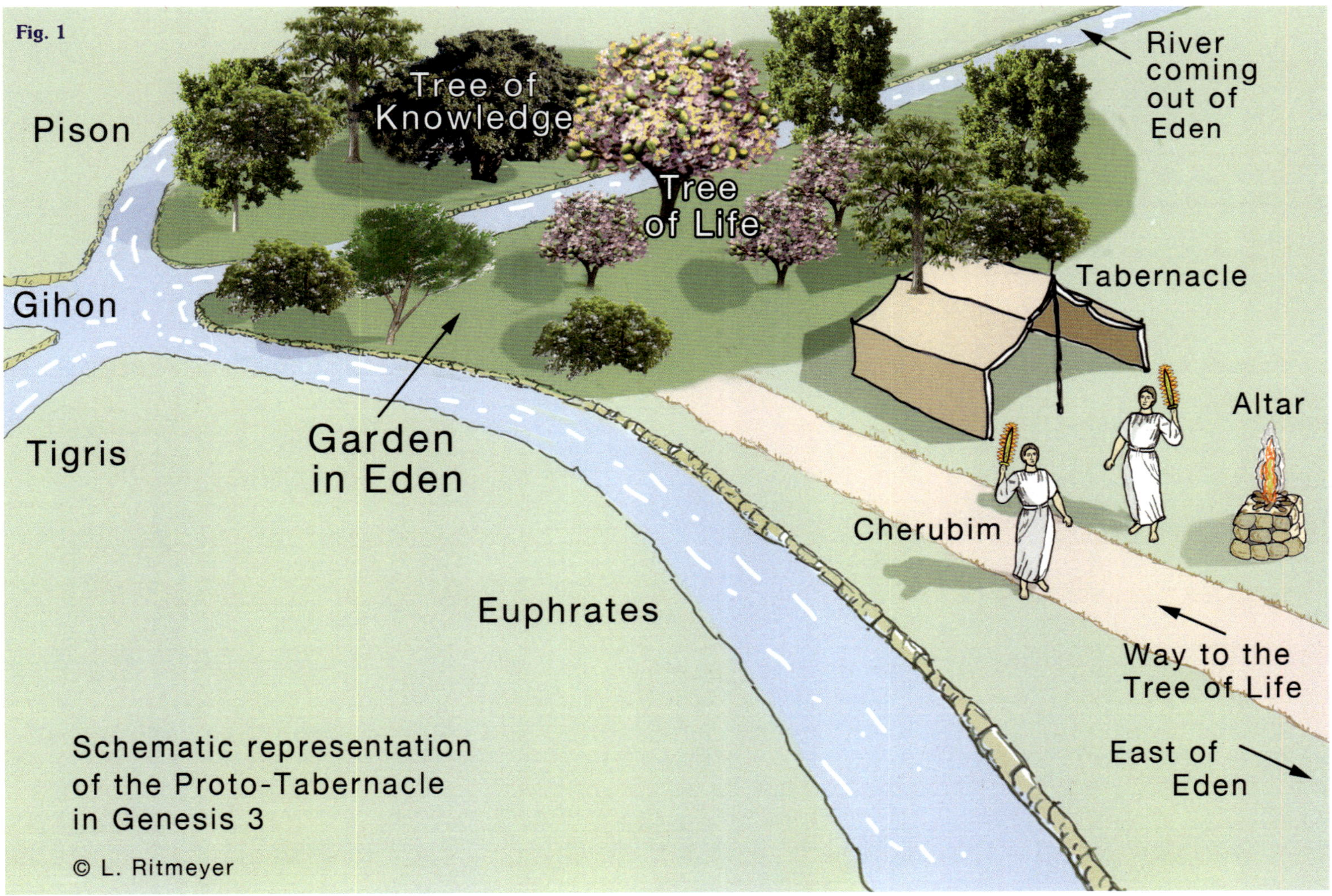

East-facing Sanctuary

The location of the sanctuary at the east side of the garden can be compared to that of the Holy Place of the later sanctuaries of Israel. The forbidden Paradise lay therefore to the west of the guarded entrance to the Garden of Eden. A road may have run from the east to an entry point or gate in a boundary that surrounded the Garden of Eden. Here the principles of worship would have been established, creating a pattern for subsequent places of worship. Anyone wanting to visit this dwelling place would have had to approach it from the east and face west. This direction of approaching a holy place from the east has been preserved in the Tabernacle and the Temple constructions, the entrances of which all faced east, while the Holy of Holies is in the west.

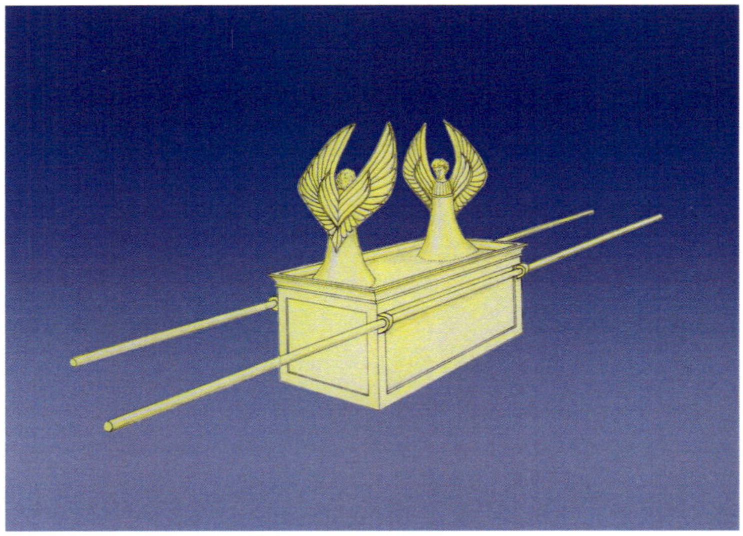

Fig. 2. *The Ark of the Covenant.*

The Altar

The principle of approaching God by sacrifice would also have been established in this place. The sword of the cherubim may have been used, not only to preserve the way to the Tree of Life by keeping humans out, but also for killing sacrifices and the flame for igniting the wood. It would be reasonable to suggest that the offerings that Cain and Abel brought to God were presented to these cherubim. Abel may have placed his offering on an altar. It was in this place that the cherubim, as divine representatives, would have taught Cain and Abel which sacrifices were acceptable and which ones were not. In the New Testament Book of Hebrews 11:4, we are told that God testified of Abel's gift. Was this testifying done by the fire of the cherubim consuming Abel's sacrifice? A similar event happened to the sacrifices brought by Gideon (Judges 6:21) and Elijah (1 Kings 18.38).

And when Cain was driven out from God's presence, he said: "from thy face (Hebrew *panim*, 'faces') shall I be hid" (Gen. 4:14). Could this be interpreted as a lament by Cain that he would be separated from seeing the faces of the cherubim, as none could see the face of God and live (Ex. 33:20)?

Fig. 3. *The inner curtains of the Tabernacle.*

Fig. 4. *The doors leading from the Holy Place into the Holy of Holies of Solomon's Temple.*

Cherubim as Priests and Guardians

The description in Genesis does not inform us as to the appearance of the cherubim, but descriptions in the Book of Exodus show that they were winged creatures and that God spoke from between them (Ex. 25:20–22; Num. 7:98). Cherubim are also mentioned in the Book of Ezekiel, but their form differs significantly from the earlier descriptions, although they perform a similar function, namely as the dwelling place or Throne of God (Ezek. 10:18).

Images of composite creatures have been found in archaeological excavations, having a body of a lion or an ox, wings like those of an eagle and a human face, are often used as examples of what the biblical cherubim may have looked like.

In the Hebrew Bible, cherubim are angel-like creatures that serve as guardians of sacred spaces and often appear in pairs. They acted as priests and guardians of the sanctuary and as mediators between God and men, as they knew which sacrifices were acceptable and which were not. They preserved the way to the Tree of Life, which, according to Rev. 2:7 represents eternal life:

> *To him that overcomes will I give to eat of the tree of life, which is in the midst of the paradise of God.*

Cherubim appear on the Ark of the Covenant **(Fig. 2)** and also on the inner curtains of the Tabernacle **(Fig. 3)**. In Solomon's Temple, cherubim were carved on the inner panels of the Holy Place (1 Kings 6:29) **(see Fig. 26)** and two massive cherubim stood over the Ark of the Covenant (1 Kings 6:23–28) **(Fig. 5)**. Cherubim were also carved on the doors leading into the Holy of Holies of Solomon's Temple (1 Kings 6:32) **(Fig. 4)**. These two doors with their cherubim appear to reflect the previous guarding duty of the cherubim in Eden. They also feature in Ezekiel's Temple (Ezek. 41:18,20,25).

The New Testament records that the inner curtain of Herod's Temple was torn from top to bottom when Christ died (Matt. 27:51; Mark 15:38; Luke 23:45). It would then have been possible to see the Holy of Holies from the Holy Place, as the separation between these chambers was destroyed. Thus the symbolic way to the Tree of Life was opened, called a "new and living way" in Hebrews 10:20.

We see in these early chapters of Genesis the basic elements of worship that formed the foundation for worship in the later sanctuaries of Israel. Later on in history, we see that faithful individuals like Noah and Abraham, Isaac and Jacob, Moses and Joshua, and many others built altars and sacrificed to God without having a sanctuary. It was only when the Tabernacle was built in Sinai that sacrifices became part of the ritual of a national sanctuary.

Fig. 5. *The Ark flanked by two large cherubim.*

MELCHIZEDEK AND ABRAHAM

In Genesis 14, we are introduced to an enigmatic personality by the name of Melchizedek. What important event brought about Melchizedek's entry into the pages of Scripture and where was Salem, the city of which he was king? The passage in Genesis 14:17 records the meeting of the patriarch Abram and the King of Sodom with Melchizedek, King of Salem, "*in the Valley of Shaveh which is the King's Dale.*" Salem could, of course, be connected etymologically to Jerusalem, but it is the undisputed location of the King's Dale (the site of the Pillar of Absalom, as described in 2 Sam. 18:18), within the confines of the city of Jerusalem, that clinches the identification. The King's Dale was an area of land in the Kedron Valley just north of the Gihon Spring **(Fig. 6)**.

The city of Salem was built next to this spring in an area today known as the City of David, south of the Temple Mount. After the victorious outcome of the battle in the north of the Land, Abram and Lot would have travelled down the Kedron Valley to meet with Melchizedek. The latter would have come down from the city of Salem that was located higher up the slopes. The extraordinary encounter would have taken place near the Gihon Spring, this being the obvious meeting place.

A Priest of the Most High God

What did Melchizedek say and what did he do?

> *And Melchizedek king of Salem brought forth bread and wine: and he was the priest of the most high God. And he blessed him, and said, Blessed be Abram of the Most High God, possessor of heaven and earth: And blessed be the most high God, which hath delivered thine enemies into thy hand. And he [Abram] gave him tithes of all.*
>
> (Gen. 14:18–20)

There is no mention of an altar, of sacrifices, holy garments, incense or a sanctuary. As priest of the Most High God, he simply brought forth bread and wine and blessed Abram.

Sacrifice on Mount Moriah

It is in the next chapter, however, in Genesis 15 ("after these things," vs. 1), that we may find the earliest reference to a sacrifice that was offered on Mount Moriah. After having met Melchizedek, it is logical to assume that Abram and his army would have stayed near Salem for a short while for the events described in Genesis 14 to have taken place. The most suitable location for his army's encampment would have been the Ophel Hill, just north of and above Salem. On this higher ground, Abram's army would have been well protected and yet near the life-giving water supply of the Gihon Spring.

From this place, God "brought him forth abroad" or "took him outside" (Gen. 15:5). God took Abram outside of his encampment and, after having given him the promise of a seed, told him to bring a sacrifice of a great number of animals. If he was camped on the Ophel Hill, the topography dictates that this sacrifice could only have taken place on Mount Moriah, north of the Ophel and the city of Melchizedek. And this act would establish this location as a holy place of huge significance in the purpose of God.

Later on in his life, Abraham, as he was now called, was told by God to go to Mount Moriah to sacrifice his only begotten son (Gen. 22). This awful request would have appeared more understandable to him if he had sacrificed there before and grasped the meaning of the place as the location where God would provide a greater sacrifice to save mankind.

We are told that Abraham built an altar on Mount Moriah (Gen. 22:9). It is commonly believed that the altar built by David was built on the same place where Abraham had bound Isaac.

Fig. 6. *The so-called King's Dale, looking northeast towards the Mount of Olives.*

THE TABERNACLE—A PORTABLE SANCTUARY

When, about 400 years later, God led the Israelites out of Egypt to bring them into the Land He had promised them, He told them that He would choose a place for His sacrifices (Deut. 12:5; 26:2, etc.). But in the meantime, the sacrificial system was to be put into operation in a portable sanctuary called the Tabernacle (*mishkan*), which they were to construct in the desert of Sinai. A detailed description of this sanctuary is found in the Book of Exodus chapters 25–40. The materials used to make and furnish the Tabernacle were provided by the Israelites who, before they left Egypt, had been given gold and silver jewelry, as well as clothing by the Egyptians[3].

The weight of gold used in the making of the Sanctuary was 29 talents and 730 shekels. The amount of silver employed was 100 talents and 1,730 shekels. The experience of working on Egyptian building projects must have produced some skilled craftsmen for this labour of love among the Israelites.

The chief craftsman of the Tabernacle was Bezalel Ben Uri, whose name appropriately means: "In the shadow of God, the son of my light." He was assisted by Aholiab: "Father's Tent," who is described as a master of the various crafts needed for the preparation of the Tabernacle.

Fig. 7 *(above). Model of the Tabernacle and enclosure.*

The Outer Courtyard

The Tabernacle itself was surrounded by an open court, formed by 60 pillars with silver capitals **(Fig. 7)**. Each pillar stood in a bronze socket and was secured by cords and tent pins made of brass. On this framework, which measured 100 by 50 cubits (172 by 86 ft. or 52.50 by 26.25 m), hung 5-cubit-high (8.5 ft. or 2.62 m) curtains of fine white linen.

The entrance to the outer court of the Tabernacle was via a curtain of fine linen interwoven with blue and purple and scarlet, supported by five pillars **(Fig. 8)**. The Altar of Burnt Offering (*mizbeach ha'olah*) and the Laver (*kior*) were the only pieces of furniture in the courtyard.

The Altar of Burnt Offering was a portable altar, made of acacia wood, 3 cubits (5 ft. or 1.50 m) high and 5 cubits (8.6 ft. or 2.60 m) long and wide. The wooden bars were overlaid with bronze and it had a bronze grating halfway up the sides, leaving space below for a fire to be made. There were bronze rings fixed on two opposite sides of the altar, so that poles for carrying it could be run through them (Ex. 27:1–8). Many utensils, such as pots, shovels, sprinkling bowls, meat forks and fire-pans were made for use by the priests when they brought animal sacrifices (Ex. 38:1–7).

Fig. 8 *(right). The courtyard of the Tabernacle, showing the Altar of Burnt Offering and the Laver.*

Fig. 9. *Entrance to the Tabernacle.*

There were four horns at the four corners of the altar and the blood of sin offerings was put on these horns (Lev. 4). These horns played an important role in the lives of people who had innocently killed another person, as taking hold of them granted them temporary immunity (Ex. 21:14). However, if the person was found guilty of murder, he could be taken away from the horns of the altar for execution, as happened to Joab (1 Kings 2:29–31).

The Laver, which was a bronze basin, was placed between the Tabernacle and the Altar. Scripture does not tell us how tall the Laver was or what it looked like, apart from the fact that it had a bronze stand (Ex. 30:18). The High Priest and his sons had to wash their hands and feet before performing their priestly duties at the Altar or in the Tabernacle (Ex. 30:18–21). From Exodus 38:8, we learn the interesting fact that the Laver and its stand were made from the mirrors of the women who served at the entrance to the Tent of Meeting. These mirrors were undoubtedly brought from Egypt, where highly polished bronze mirrors were used at that time.

The Tabernacle Structure

Moses was commanded to make the Tabernacle according to the pattern shown to him on the mount (Ex. 25:40). As the tents of the children of Israel were movable, so the Sanctuary that God commanded to be made for him could also be dismantled, transported and then re-erected.

The entrance to the Tabernacle **(Fig. 9)** was via a curtain of fine linen interwoven with blue and purple and scarlet, suspended from the tops of five gold-covered pillars (Ex. 26:36–37). The entrance was on the east, and this east-facing direction, which originated in the Genesis sanctuary, was followed in the later temples that were built on Mount Moriah.

According to Exodus 26:15–30, the Tabernacle itself was made of boards of shittim wood overlaid with gold along three of its sides and was 30 cubits (52 ft. or 15.75 m) long and 10 cubits (17 ft. or 5.25 m) wide. The shittah tree (plural, shittim) is now called the acacia or wattle and is the most characteristic tree of the Sinai desert. In this area, these trees never grew as tall as the boards from which the Tabernacle was made **(Fig. 10)**. It would appear therefore that these boards and other large items, such as the Ark of the Covenant and the pillars of the Tabernacle, must have been made up of several timbers joined together. The boards rested on silver sockets, with two sockets placed under each board. The boards each had two tenons or projections (Hebrew: *yadot*, "hands") at the bottom and the sockets had corresponding holes in them, so that both items could be securely fixed. The boards were held upright by bars that traversed each of the three sides. Cords attached to the ground with brass pins further ensured its stability. The entire structure was covered over with four layers of coverings (Ex. 26:1–14). Fine linen, interwoven with blue, purple and scarlet and embroidered with cherubim, formed the ceiling of the Tabernacle. On top of this were laid coverings made of goat's hair, then rams' skins dyed red and finally what is most frequently translated as badgers' skins (*tachashim*). This latter cover is variously translated as made of sealskins, hides of sea cows, goat skins, etc., testifying to the difficulty of identifying what material was used as the outer cover of the Tabernacle. The interior of the Tabernacle consisted of two chambers, separated by a curtain.

The Holy Place

The first chamber **(see Fig. 3)**, called the Holy Place (*kodesh*), was 20 cubits (34 ft. or 10.50 m) long and 10 cubits wide (17 ft. or 5.25 m). On both sides the golden boards, which rested on silver sockets, were visible. The Veil (*parokhet*) was supported by four pillars and separated the Holy from the Holy of Holies (*kodesh hakodashim*). It was made of linen and decorated with embroidered cherubim. In front of the Veil stood the Altar of Incense (*mizbeach haketoret*), which was attended to twice a day. On the south side stood the Lampstand (*menorah*) that was modeled on a flowering almond tree, with cups looking like almond flowers and blossoms decorating the branches (Ex. 25:33,34; 37:19,20). It was crafted out of a talent of pure gold, which was about the weight of a man. A central stem with three branches on both its sides created a seven-branched Lampstand, with each of the branches holding a golden lamp. The lamps were lit daily using pure olive oil and burned from evening to morning (Ex. 27:20,21).

The Table for the Shewbread (*shulchan lehem hapanim*) was placed on the north side, in an east-west orientation. It was made

Fig. 10. *Photograph of Leen Ritmeyer, one of the authors, under an acacia tree, showing the relative size of a board of the Tabernacle.*

of shittim wood and overlaid with gold. Two rows or piles of loaves of unleavened bread were placed on the table with golden dishes for incense. These were called the shewbread, but the Hebrew (*lechem hapanim*) literally means "Bread of Faces." This is understood to mean that each loaf of bread represented one of the tribes of Israel with their "faces" lifted up towards God. The main ritual of the Sanctuary associated with the Sabbath in Scripture was the changing of the twelve loaves on the Table of Shewbread (Lev. 24:5–9).

Fig. 11. *Interior view of the Holy of Holies.*

The Holy of Holies

The inner sanctuary, called the Holy of Holies, or *debir*, was cube-shaped, with each side measuring 10 cubits (17 ft. or 5.25 m). As in the Holy Place, the golden boards, which rested on silver sockets, could be seen. Similarly, the ceiling, made of fine linen, interwoven with blue, purple and scarlet and with embroidered cherubim, was visible from the inside **(Fig. 11 left)**.

Only the High Priest (*hakohen hagadol*), could enter the Holy of Holies once a year on the Day of Atonement (*Yom Kippur*). In the center of the Holy of Holies stood the Ark of the Covenant.

The Ark of the Covenant

Although in this publication, we have first described the Tabernacle, in Scripture, the Ark of the Covenant was the first item that God commanded the Israelites to make (Ex. 25:10–22) **(Fig. 12)**. The specifications of the remainder of the furniture and the Tabernacle came afterwards. The Ark was undoubtedly the most holy piece of furniture ever made. It consisted of a rectangular chest, 2.5 cubits long and 1.5 cubits broad and high (4.3 ft. and 2.6 ft. or 1.31 m and 0.79 m), made of shittim wood and overlaid inside and outside with gold (Ex. 25:10,11). An ornamental border that went around the top of the Ark is called the "crown of gold" (*zer zahav*). The lid of the Ark was also made of pure gold and was known as the Mercy-seat (*kapporet*). Rising out of the two sides of this Mercy-seat and beaten out of the same piece of gold were the Cherubim (*keruvim*), winged figures whose faces looked towards the Mercy-seat and whose wings overshadowed it[4].

The word for Ark (*aron*) in Hebrew means merely a chest and has been translated as "coffin" in Genesis 50:26. When the Ark was first made, it contained only the two tablets of stone on which God had engraved the Ten Commandments (Ex. 25:16). From the Book of Hebrews 9:4, however, we learn that two other items were also placed inside the Ark—a golden pot filled with manna, the food God provided for the Israelites during their forty years in the Wilderness, and the almond rod that budded miraculously, proving that the selection of Aaron as High Priest was divinely appointed. This record does not specify when these two items were added but would indicate that it was at some time during the wilderness journey. Just before his death (Deut. 31:24–26), Moses was commanded to write a scroll of laws (probably the Deuteronomy Scroll) and place it by the side of the Ark.

Fig. 12. *The Ark of the Covenant.*

Two staves, also made of shittim wood and covered with gold, were slotted through golden rings, so that the Ark could be moved from one place to another. Scripture does not give the length of these staves, but a Talmudic reference (*Yoma* 54a) states that they were 10 cubits (17.2 ft. or 5.25 m) long. They could not have been longer as otherwise the Ark of the Covenant with the staves would not have fitted inside the Holy of Holies, which measured 10 cubits square.

The Ark with its golden covering and its cherubim were the seat of the Deity and from this place God spoke to Moses:

There I will meet with thee, and I will commune with thee from above the mercy seat, from between the two cherubim which are upon the ark of the testimony, of all things which I will give thee in commandment unto the children of Israel. (Ex. 25:22)

Degrees of Holiness

In the Tabernacle compound **(Fig. 13)**, we see a tripartite structure with ascending degrees of holiness from the Outer Courtyard to the Holy Place and finally to the Holy of Holies. Initially, Israelites were allowed in the courtyard to bring their sacrifices, but only priests were allowed to serve in the Holy Place. The Holy of Holies was the most restricted place, reserved for a once-yearly entry by the High Priest.

This pattern, which was divinely inspired and shown to Moses in the mount (Ex. 25:40), became the pattern for the construction of the subsequent temples.

Fig. 13. *The Tabernacle compound.*

The Tabernacle served as the only sanctuary for Israel and travelled with them through the desert wanderings. On entering the Land, it stood for many years at Shiloh, but later moved to Gibeon, from whence Solomon brought it up to Jerusalem and stored it in one of the side chambers of the Temple (1 Kings 8:4; 2 Chron. 5:5).

The High Priest

The first High Priest was Moses' brother Aaron, with the succession going through his male descendants (Ex. 28:1). The sons of Aaron, Nadab and Abihu, Eleazar and Ithamar, assisted him with the daily tasks.

The High Priest was attired in elaborate vestments, which had been specially prepared by "gifted artisans…filled with the spirit of wisdom," while camped under Sinai. The garments were designed "for glory and for beauty" and described in Exodus 28. Describing these vestments **(Fig. 14)** beginning from the front, the High Priest wore the ephod that was a kind of apron, made of white, blue, purple and scarlet, and embroidered with gold threads. The ephod was tied with a waistband and had two shoulder pieces. These shoulder pieces each held an onyx stone set in gold and engraved with the names of the tribes of Israel. The breastplate of judgment (*hoshen hamishpat*) was composed of twelve precious stones in four rows of three, each representing one of the twelve tribes. It also contained the "Urim and Thummim" (Lights and Perfections), which were used to ascertain the divine will. Under the ephod went a blue robe from the hem of which hung pomegranates of blue, purple and scarlet, alternating with golden bells. A coat made of fine linen was worn under the robe. Finally, the gold frontlet (*ziz*), worn on the head of the High Priest, symbolized the holiness that he was supposed to manifest to God and bore the words "Holiness to Yahweh."

The most important function of the High Priest was his service on *Yom Kippur*—the Day of Atonement (see below). On regular days, the High Priest was assisted by his sons in the daily duties of the Tabernacle, such as the offering of the daily sacrifice, the offering of incense and the care of the Lampstand and the Table of Shewbread. The Levites were assigned the task of moving the Tabernacle in its journeys.

The Service of the Tabernacle

The worship of God in the Tabernacle laid the foundation for the worship of the subsequent Temples. In the outer court, two lambs were sacrificed each day on the Altar of Burnt Sacrifices, one in the morning and one in the evening. Inside the Holy Place of the Tabernacle, incense was burnt on the Altar of Incense also twice a day, while in the evening the lights of the Lampstand were lit.

Fig. 14. *The High Priest.*

In the Book of Leviticus, many other sacrifices are mentioned, but the main ones all fell under the heading of one of the four following offerings: the burnt offerings, the sin offerings, the trespass offerings and the peace offerings **(see chart, opposite)**.

The burnt offering was offered when there was no particular offense but to atone for the unclean state of human nature. As regards the sin offering, public offerings of this kind were always male animals, while private offerings could be female. As the name implies, the trespass offering was needful in cases of disobedience against a specific law. Finally, the peace offerings also had to be a living creature for sacrifice, but offered out of pure love at the completion of other sacrifices.

The Feasts of Israel

The Feasts of Israel, described principally in Leviticus 23 and Deuteronomy 16, feature prominently in the Temple services, but they were instituted at the foot of Mount Sinai, where the Israelites were encamped during that first year after they had left Egypt and were instructed to make the Tabernacle. During the desert wanderings, the Israelites ate manna, as it was impossible to grow crops. Most of the Feasts of Israel are connected with the harvest and could therefore only be fully kept when the Israelites arrived in the Land. The Tabernacle then became the focus where the three main feasts were observed, as stipulated in Exodus 23:14 "Three times thou shalt keep a feast unto me in the year." These refer to the three joyful festivals of Passover (*Pesach*), Weeks (*Shavuot*) and Tabernacles (*Succot*). Other feasts were introduced later in the history of the Temple, but it was these three that remained as pilgrim festivals, when it was enjoined on all male Israelites to travel to Jerusalem to keep them.

The Sabbath (*Shabbat*)

In Leviticus 23 the feasts that were to be kept by the Israelites begin with the injunction to keep the seventh day of the week holy. No work was to be done on the holy Sabbath. Each individual had to rest on that last day of the week, apart from the priests that officiated in the Tabernacle. The main ritual of the Sanctuary associated with the Sabbath in Scripture was the changing of the twelve loaves of shewbread on the Table of Shewbread (Lev. 24:5–9). In Numbers 28:9–10, we read that two lambs, along with the meal and drink offering, be offered as a special Sabbath offering.

The Feast of Passover (*Pesach*)

The feast of Passover (*Pesach*) took place during one of the months whose original

MAIN OFFERINGS

BURNT *(OLAH)*:
The entire surrender to God of an individual or the congregation

SIN *(CHATAT)*:
To make atonement for the person of the offender—to cover our sinful nature

TRESPASS *(ASHAM)*:
To make atonement for a specific offence done in ignorance

PEACE *(SHELAMIM)*:
To complete other sacrifices which always preceded it

biblical name Abib has come down to us (Ex. 13:4). The Scripture records that it was to be to the Israelites their "beginning of months" (Ex. 12:2), which would commence the sacred year. A lamb had to be offered on the 14th day of that first month, followed by one week of eating unleavened bread. In a historical sense, it was an annual celebration of their deliverance from Egyptian bondage and the birth of Israel as a nation. The name *pesach* means to "pass over" or "step over" and refers to how the Angel of Death passed over the houses of the Israelites as he slew the firstborn of the Egyptians (Ex. 12:27). The Passover sacrifice was therefore initially not a Levitical sacrifice, but one that was instituted earlier in Egypt. Even earlier than that, in Abraham's sacrifice recorded in Genesis 15, we have a foreshadowing of the Passover, with the phrase "in the self-same day" mentioned in Genesis 15:18, being picked up in Exodus 12:41:

> *And it came to pass at the end of the four-hundred-and-thirty years, even the self-same day it came to pass, that all the hosts of the LORD went out from the land of Egypt.*

In Leviticus 23, the description of the Passover is immediately followed by the injunction to bring a sheaf (Hebrew, *omer*—a container holding about 5.1 pints) of the firstfruits of their harvest to the priest on the day after the Sabbath and raise it up. The waving of the *omer* began the countdown to the next feast, the Feast of Weeks (*Shavuot*), or Pentecost, as it is known in the New Testament.

The Feast of Weeks (*Shavuot*)

Fifty days had to be counted from the Sabbath preceding the raising of the *omer*. The name *Shavuot* derives from the seven Sabbaths, i.e., seven weeks, that had to be completed until this next feast. Again, on the first day of the week, two barley loaves that were baked with leaven were offered, together with seven lambs, one bull, two rams and a goat for a sin offering. Being of agricultural significance, this feast could only be observed once they had entered the Land and were able to lead a settled existence.

The Jewish New Year (*Rosh Hashanah*)

The third of the great festivals, the Feast of Tabernacles (*Succot*), fell in the seventh month, the month of *Tishrei*. This month is a time of year corresponding to September/October in the Northern Hemisphere when the days grow shorter and the clouds begin to gather in preparation for the early rain or *yoreh* that starts the rainy season. There is activity in plant life almost equal to the Spring with the ripening of olives, dates, grapes, figs and pomegranates. The first day of the seventh month was the New Year (*Rosh Hashanah*). Scripture describes this feast as: "a Sabbath, a memorial of blowing of trumpets, an holy convocation" (Lev. 23:24) and as: "a blowing of trumpets" (Num. 29:1). This was because the blowing of trumpets or *shofars* was a major feature of the feast. However, the Mishnah (*Rosh Hashanah* 3:3–4) makes it clear that it was not the usual silver trumpets (*chatzotzrot*) that were used but animal horns: "The *shofar* used in the Temple at the New Year was made from the horn of the wild goat, straight, with its mouthpiece overlaid with gold." This was blown between a pair of silver trumpets, with the *shofar* as the main instrument of the day giving a long note and the latter a short one. Apart from the blowing of the *shofar*, the only other injunction for *Rosh Hashanah* was the offering of sacrifices. These comprised a special festive offering of a young bullock, a ram and seven lambs, in addition to the usual morning and evening sacrifices and the burnt offering of the regular new moon.

The Day of Atonement (*Yom Kippur*)

The feast of blowing of trumpets was followed ten days later by the Day of Atonement. This period between the two feasts was a time of penitence in preparation for the most solemn day in the Jewish calendar. The Scriptural injunction then for the 10th of *Tishrei* was that: "it shall be an holy convocation unto you; and ye shall afflict your souls, and offer an offering made by fire unto the Lord. And you shall do no work in that same day: for it is a day of atonement, to make an atonement for you before the Lord your God" (Lev. 23:27,28). The most solemn part of the day's service was the annual entrance of the High Priest into the Holy of Holies. On this occasion, he was not dressed in his usual brightly colored garments, but in robes of white linen. He took burning coals on his fire-pan and with a ladle carrying two handfuls of incense, he entered into the Holy of Holies and also sprinkled the blood of a bullock, his personal sacrifice, in front of the mercy-seat of the Ark of the Covenant. On that same day, a scapegoat (*azazel*) was chosen from among two goats. The High Priest confessed over him the sins of the people of Israel and then the scapegoat was led into the wilderness (Lev. 16).

The Feast of Tabernacles (*Succot*)

The Feast of Tabernacles began on the 15th of *Tishrei* and continued until the 21st of the month, when it was followed by the Feast of the Eighth Day. Once in the Land, the entire population had to obey the commandment, "ye shall dwell in booths (*succot*) seven days, all that are Israelites born shall dwell in booths" (Lev. 23: 42). In Leviticus 23:40, four kinds of trees are mentioned in the commandments for the Feast of Tabernacles: "the boughs of goodly trees, branches of palm trees, and the boughs of thick trees, and willows of the brook."

The use to which these branches were to be put was not made clear, and later in Jewish tradition, was interpreted either as a list of materials from which the booths should be made or as a list of items to be carried in the hands. Apart from the dwelling in booths, there were distinctive sacrifices associated with the festival. Numbers 29:12–40 enumerates the offerings for the first day of the feast and the following six days, each of which had their own offerings. Each day, the burnt offerings consisted of fourteen lambs, two rams and one goat, with their corresponding meal and drink offerings. In addition, there was an offering of bullocks, whose number decreased every day, so that on the first day of the feast, thirteen bullocks were offered, while on the last day only seven. On the eighth day or octave, they were to have: "a solemn assembly" (vs. 35) and a single bullock was offered.

THE JOURNEYS OF THE TABERNACLE

With the stern jagged peak of Horeb, from which God spoke as its backdrop, the four-sided camp stood on the plain in the divinely prescribed order. Each side of the encampment was shared by three tribes under the standard of the leading tribe for that group. Thus, Judah, Issachar and Zebulon camped on the east side under the standard of Judah. Reuben, Simeon and Gad were on the south side under the standard of Reuben. On the west side were Ephraim, Manasseh and Benjamin under the standard of Ephraim, while on the north were the tribes of Dan, Asher and Naphtali under the standard of Dan.

Inside this sea of tents was a narrow line of tents which belonged to the priestly families. On the east were those of Moses and Aaron, while on the south was the family of Kohath. The family of Gershon encamped on the west, while the family of Merari had their row of tents in the north. All these surrounded the Tabernacle, the movable sanctuary, over which rested a pillar of cloud that shaded the entire camp from the intense desert sun (Ps. 105:39).

The Camp of Israel

It was of course only at the end of their sojourn under the mountain that the wonderful order shown in this portrayal of the encampment was attained **(Fig. 15)**. The record in Exodus 40:17 tells us that the Tabernacle was "raised up" in the first month of the second year of their stay in Sinai, whereas Numbers 10:11,12, gives us the date on which they left this spot: the twentieth day of the second month. Sometime during this seven-week period, as recorded in Numbers 2, the Israelites were transformed from a shapeless mass of people into a nation whose progress through the desert was prescribed down to the minutest detail and whose discipline would be the envy of the sternest military commander. From a scene such as this, the Tabernacle commenced its wanderings[5].

The Wilderness Wanderings

God indicated to the Israelites that they were to march by taking up the cloud that covered the Tabernacle. The order in which they moved was also divinely appointed. First went the camp of Judah, then the sons of Gershon and Merari carrying the various items that made up the Tabernacle structure with the curtains and hangings for the court. The camp of the Reubenites followed. The Kohathites then set forward carrying the vessels of the Sanctuary, including the Ark. The Levites carried the Ark on their shoulders by means of two long staves. The staves were left in the rings so as always to be ready at a moment's notice for the next journey. The camp of Ephraim and then of Dan followed after the vessels of the Sanctuary. Upon arrival at another site, the camp was pitched in its prescribed order, with the Tabernacle set up in readiness to receive the Ark.

On two occasions, however, this order was changed. When Israel first departed from Mount Sinai, we read that: "the ark of the covenant of the Lord went before them in a three days' journey, to search out a resting place for them" (Num. 10:33). The other time we read of the Ark leading the children of Israel was when they

Fig. 15. *The encampment of Israel around the Tabernacle at the foot of Mount Horeb.*

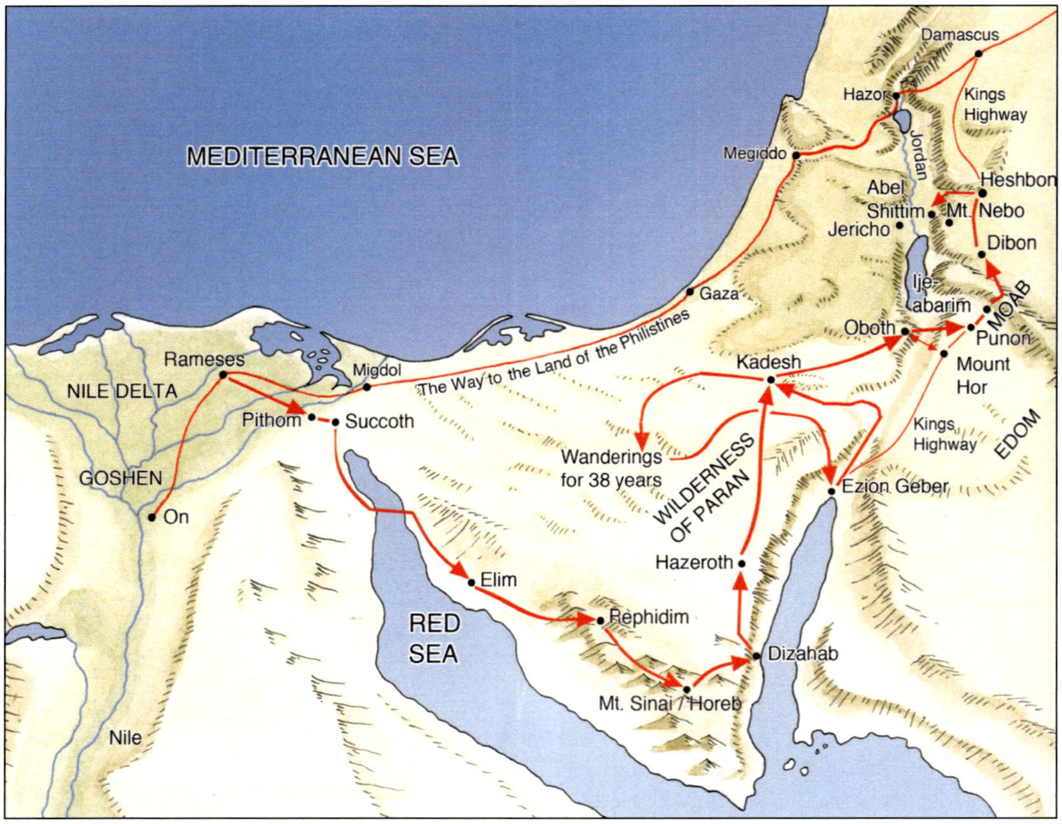

Fig. 16. *The traditional route of the Exodus.*

crossed the river Jordan to go into the Promised Land.

We can identify with certainty only the main stations of the journey recorded in the earlier part of the Book of Numbers, Hazeroth and Kadesh **(Fig. 16)**. Most of the sites mentioned in the detailed itinerary given in Numbers 33:16–49 are untraceable today, as the names given to these sites by the Israelites often refer to events they were involved in and would not be preserved in the names given them by the local Bedouin.

We are told that it was eleven days' journey from Horeb to Kadesh-barnea (Deut. 1:2). It would be a mistake however to assume that they went directly to Kadesh from Mount Sinai. They left the mountain where they had received God's laws in the second month of the second year (Num. 10:11) and appear to have taken almost a year to reach Kadesh (Deut. 2:14). This delay accords well with a detour over to the coast of the Gulf of Aqaba necessitated by a verse in Deuteronomy 1:1, which has Moses speaking to the children of Israel, "in the plain opposite Suph (the Red Sea), between Paran, Tophel, Laban, and Hazeroth, and Dizahab." Dizahab is almost universally identified with the present-day Dahab on the east coast of the Sinai peninsula, about 47 miles or 75 km from Mount Sinai **(see Fig. 16)**.

From here, they would have journeyed inland to Hazeroth, where they stayed for at least seven days, the period for which Miriam was shut out of the camp with leprosy (Num. 12:15). Their journey then brought them into the Wilderness of Paran (the name apparently given to the desert of the Sinai peninsula), and the record in Numbers 13:26 leads to Kadesh-barnea. This is almost universally taken to be the site that is known today as Ein el-Qudeirat, a lush oasis with a copious spring in the northern Negev. They had now reached the border of the Promised Land and twelve spies (one for each tribe) were sent to report on conditions there. Because of the lack of faith evident in their report, despite the encouragement of Joshua and Caleb, they were prevented from entering the Land and left to wander in the desert for the next thirty-eight years.

Towards the end of their wanderings, they appear from the itinerary in Numbers 33 to have returned to Kadesh via Ezion-geber, present-day Eilat, at the head of the Gulf of Aqaba. Moses requested permission from the King of Edom to pass by the King's Highway but was refused. They then passed on to Mount Hor, where Aaron was buried. The route then goes from Mount Hor to Zalmonah, Punon, Oboth, Ije-abarim on the border of Moab, Dibon-gad, Almon-diblathaim, and to the mountains of Abarim before descending to the Plains of Moab by the Jordan near Jericho. It was here that the Israelites set up their last camp in preparation for the assault on Canaan and here Moses gave his last discourses to the people of Israel **(Fig. 17)**.

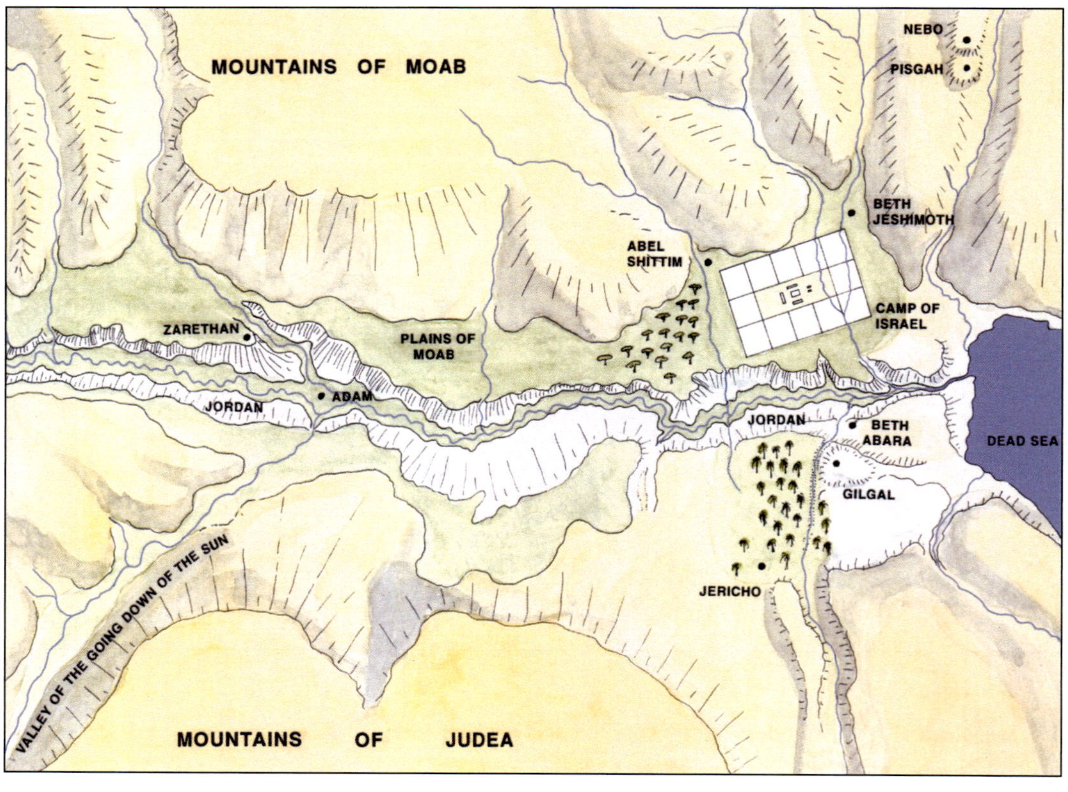

Fig. 17. *Camp of the Israelites on the Plains of Moab.*

This site was the last of the forty-five stations enumerated in Numbers 33. Here it is recorded:

They departed from the mountains of Abarim and camped in the plains of Moab by the Jordan, across from Jericho. They camped by the Jordan, from Beth-jesimoth as far as the Abel Acacia Grove (Abel-shittim) in the plains of Moab. (vss. 48,49)

The sites of Abel-shittim and Beth-jesimoth would have been located here at either end of this well-irrigated stretch of plain bordering the east bank of the Jordan. This dramatic view of the Israelites poised for the long-awaited entry to the Promised Land formed part of the panorama seen first by Balaam, and shortly afterwards by Moses, from the lofty mountaintops above. Balaam, a Mesopotamian prophet, was hired by Balak king of Moab to curse the Israelites, but was compelled by God to bless them instead. Moses' view, by contrast, was imbued by faith and he envisioned the future inheritance of his people, although he himself was not allowed to enter the Promised Land. He was buried by an angel in a valley below the plateau of Nebo, but the exact place of his burial is unknown.

After crossing the river Jordan, the Israelites set up camp in Gilgal on the east border of Jericho. The Tabernacle was set up here and the Feast of Passover observed (Josh. 5:10).

In the Promised Land

During the long wars waged by the Israelites against the Canaanites in the heartland of the country, the Tabernacle and the Ark stayed in Gilgal. Then, in Joshua 18:1, we read:

the whole congregation of the children of Israel assembled together at Shiloh and set up the tabernacle of meeting there.

Shiloh is the most meticulously defined place in the whole of Scripture, with a verse at the end of the Book of Judges (21:19) describing its location as:

on the north side of Beth-el, on the east side of the highway that goeth up from Beth-el to Shechem, and on the south of Lebonah.

A tell called Seilun in the hill-country of Ephraim preserved the name of Shiloh, while a nearby village called Luvan preserved the name of Levonah. Excavations at Shiloh have revealed a Middle Bronze Age (Canaanite) city wall and glacis. Pillared buildings dating from the Iron Age or Early Israelite period were found built against this city wall. It was most probably the very seclusion of this site that determined its choice as the new site of the Tabernacle. Here the allotment of territory to the various tribes could proceed unhampered by interference by the Canaanites who still held large areas in their possession farther to the north and south.

Shiloh later became the permanent seat of the priesthood. The story of Hannah and Samuel in the first chapters of the Book of Samuel takes place against the background of Eli as High Priest. From these chapters, we get the impression that the Tabernacle was kept in some sort of permanent structure referred to as the "house of the LORD" (Hebrew, *bayit Yahweh*) (1 Sam. 1:7,24, etc.), in contrast to the movable structure that was continually erected and dismantled during the wilderness wanderings. The Mishnah says as much: "After they came to Shiloh, the high places were forbidden. There was no roof-beam there, but below was a house of stone and above were hangings and this was the 'resting place'" (*Zebachim* 14:6).

Among the Philistines

While the newly arrived Israelites were establishing their settlements in the hill-country, with Shiloh as their civic center, the Philisines, also newly arrived, from the Aegean, were settling on the coastal plain.

Aphek, where the Philistines assembled for their notable battle with the Israelites, was the place where the drama began which sent the Holy Ark on seven months of wandering through enemy territory until the damage it inflicted was so great that it was sent away.

The site of Aphek marked the northern border of the Philistines and was very strong strategically. It guarded the road from the coastal plain to the hill-country where the Israelites had settled. The battle waged here was one of many in the constant struggle between the Israelites and the Philistines over control of the country's key routes. Aphek also lies near the source of the river Yarkon that flows into the Mediterranean Sea near present-day Tel Aviv.

The exact location of Ebenezer, where the Israelites assembled for battle, is unclear but it is thought to have been east of Aphek on the edge of the Judean foothills. A site known as Izbet Sartah, perched on one of these hills overlooking Aphek, has been identified as a possible rallying place of the Israelites. Defeat seemed inevitable from the outset. When four thousand Israelites fell on the first day, the elders sent for the Ark of the Covenant in Shiloh to help lead them in battle. Although terror had seized the army of the Philistines, they were still victorious, completely routing the Israelites. The news that the battle had been lost and the Ark taken into captivity brought Eli to his death (1 Sam. 4). Although it is not recorded in the biblical narrative, it would appear from other references in the Scripture that the Philistines then proceeded to Shiloh, destroying it completely. The prophet Jeremiah records the destruction of Shiloh in order to warn the people of this time to mend their ways: "But go ye now unto my place which was in Shiloh, where I did set my house at the first and see what I did to it for the wickedness of my people Israel" (Jer. 7:12).

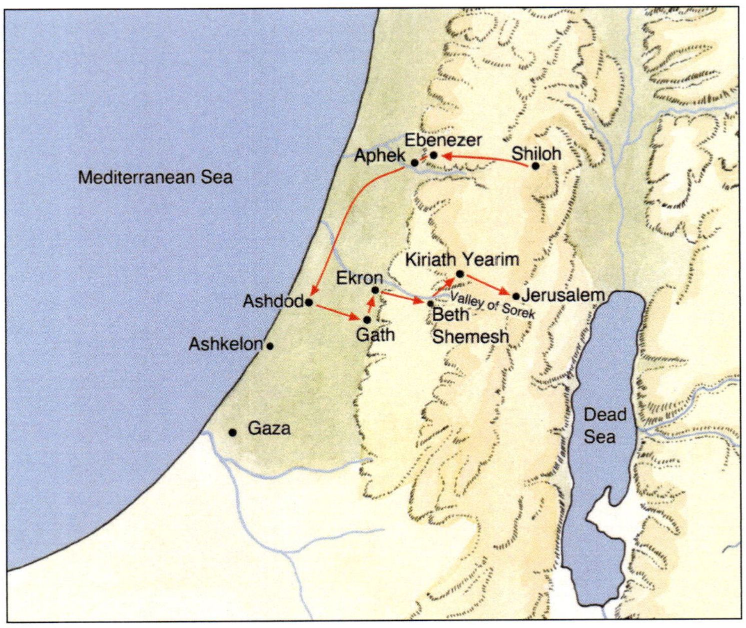

Fig. 18. *Wanderings of the Ark of the Covenant.*

The Scriptural record of the wanderings of the Ark among the Philistines **(Fig. 18)** provides a vivid picture of the Philistine region on the coastal plain. Its fertility and proximity to the sea must have attracted these seafarers to this low-lying area. However, of all the five cities of the Philistine Pentapolis, Ashkelon is the only one situated on the seashore. The Ark was first taken to Ashdod, a large, heavily fortified city about 3 miles or 5 km south of the present-day city of the same name. Here, the fish-god Dagon, originally a Canaanite deity, was worshipped in his own temple. The Ark, however, brought only trouble to its captors. The first calamity to befall the Philistines was the toppling of Dagon's image when the Ark was placed alongside him. The fact that the Philistines placed the Ark in their great cultic center shows that they held it in great reverence.

The downfall of their idol was followed by a plague of "tumors" (1 Sam. 5:6), thought to be bubonic plague, in the city and the surrounding area. The terrified Ashdodites lost no time in sending the Ark inland to Gath which commanded the entrance to the Valley of Elah on the borders of Israelite territory. Here too the plague broke out. In desperation, the Philistines sent the Ark to Ekron, the Philistine town nearest to the territory of Israel. It was from here that the Ark was returned to Israel, by the pass that led up to Beth-shemesh in the Judean foothills or Shephelah.

Unguided by human hand, two milking cows left their calves to pull a cart bearing the Ark behind them up the Valley of Sorek. After seven eventful months, the Ark had now left the country of the Philistines. The power of the Philistines and the necessity for strong opposition paved the way for the choosing of Israel's first king, Saul.

On the Way to Jerusalem

The Ark was not to remain here in the foothills, which was at this time disputed territory between the Philistines and the Israelites. Some of the men of Beth-shemesh, after their initial jubilation at the arrival of the Ark, failed to accord it proper respect, with the result that 50,070 men were destroyed. Reacting just as did the Philistines, the terror-stricken Beth-shemites sought to rid themselves of the Ark's fearsome power: "Who is able to stand before this holy LORD God? And to whom shall it go up from us" (1 Sam. 6:20). The men of Beth-shemesh asked the people of Kiriath-jearim to come and look after the Ark, which they did (1 Sam. 7:1). This place was the nearest town in the hill-country and although it belonged to the Gibeonites, who were of Canaanite origin, it was in territory that was at that time conceded to Israel. During the Ark's twenty-year sojourn on the hill, it was attended by a properly sanctified guardian—Eleazar, the son of Abinadab—in whose house the Ark was put for safe-keeping.

The twenty years that the Ark was secluded in Kiriath-jearim corresponded to the thirteen-year reign of Saul and the seven-year reign of David in Hebron (2 Sam. 5:5). All the time when David was fleeing and then reigning in Hebron, he dreamed of bringing up the Ark. One of the first things he did when he came up to Jerusalem was to go to Kiriath-jearim, intending to bring the Ark up to the city in which he now reigned over Israel **(Fig. 19)**. When David had the Ark removed from Kiriath-jearim, he did not follow the Scriptural stipulation that the Ark be carried by its staves on the shoulders of Kohathite priests. It was again placed on a cart driven by Ahio, son of Abinadab. Somewhere between Kiriath-jearim and Jerusalem, they paid the price for the violation of the divinely prescribed procedure

Fig. 19. *Kiriath-jearim today.*

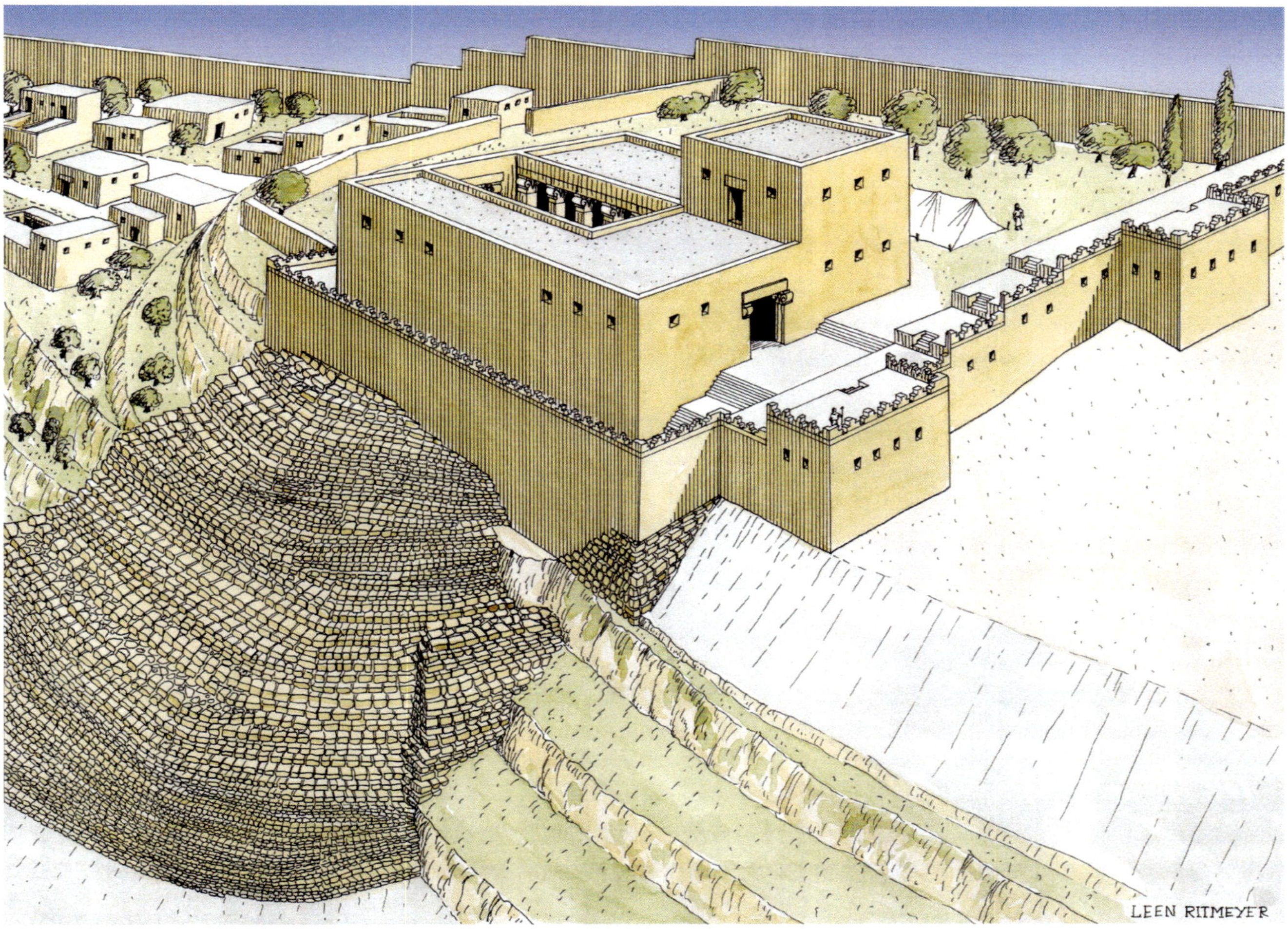

Fig. 20. *Reconstruction drawing of David's palace.*

of transporting this holy object. At the threshing-floor of Nachon (2 Sam. 6:6 and 1 Chron. 13:9, where his name is given as Chidon), on the lower slopes of one of the rounded hills on the way, Uzzah touched the Ark in an attempt to steady it and was struck down instantly. This tragedy caused King David to change his mind about bringing the Ark up to the City of David. Instead, it was brought into a nearby house, again that of a Gentile, Obed-edom the Gittite" (2 Sam. 6:10), where it stayed for another three months. When David saw that the house of Obed-edom was blessed by God, he regained his confidence and brought up the Ark to Jerusalem.

There can rarely have been such a joyful occasion as the bringing up of the Ark into Jerusalem. Two whole chapters of the first book of Chronicles (15 and 16) are devoted to its description. This time the Ark was carried by the staves on the shoulders of the Levites, as David said "for because you did it not the first time, the LORD our God broke out against us, because we did not consult Him about the proper order" (1 Chron. 15:13). The musical instruments that accompanied the singing Levites are carefully enumerated, as is the fact that the elders of Israel and the military captains were part of the procession. In fact, the record describes "all Israel" (1 Chron. 15:28) as involved in the ceremony. However, it is the picture of David's utter joy as expressed in his dancing that stands out in this account (also 2 Sam. 6:14,15). David placed the Ark in a tent, presumably near his palace **(Fig. 20)** where there would have been space to accommodate large gatherings and offered burnt offerings and peace offerings before the Lord (2 Sam. 6:17).

The Ark had now arrived at its last station before its installation in the Holy of Holies of the Temple, built by Solomon, David's son.

DAVID'S ALTAR ON MOUNT MORIAH

The last pre-Israelite ruler of Jerusalem was Araunah the Jebusite. At that time, the mountain was used for growing wheat and barley, as indicated by the reference to the threshing floor of Araunah in 1 Chronicles 21:15. After God had brought a plague on Israel, the angel of the Lord, who was about to destroy Jerusalem, told King David to build an altar on the threshing floor. The angel was standing on higher ground, between heaven and earth as it were, most likely at the peak of Mount Moriah, while the threshing floor was on slightly lower ground to the east, to exploit the prevailing westerly winds to separate the chaff from the grain. Threshing floors are never located on the very top of mountains, as the strong westerly wind would blow away both chaff and grain, but always on lower ground, usually on the eastern side. As mentioned earlier, Jewish tradition maintains that David's altar was built (c. 980 B.C.) on the same place that Abraham had erected his altar in preparation for the sacrifice of Isaac, before God intervened.

David was not allowed to build a temple and the Ark of the Covenant was now separated from the Tabernacle. At some point in time, the tabernacle must have been moved from Shiloh to a place nearer Jerusalem, namely Gibeon. There were now two places of worship, the Tabernacle in Gibeon and the Ark of the Covenant in the City of David. Eventually both were reunited when they were housed in the Temple of Solomon.

SOLOMON'S TEMPLE

In accordance with the biblical injunction, the Temple in Jerusalem eventually became the sole place for sacrifices and important religious meetings. In the Book of Deuteronomy there are nineteen references to this particular place of which Moses was told in advance. Deuteronomy 12:5 is the first of these, directing the Israelites exclusively

unto the place which the LORD your God shall choose out of all your tribes to put his name there, even unto his habitation shall ye seek, and thither thou shalt come.

The many reconstruction drawings that have been made of Solomon's Temple are usually based on the artist's personal interpretation of the biblical text. Some designs are more fanciful than others and often use contemporary architectural styles for the decoration of the building[6].

The reconstructions we will attempt here are the first based on archaeological evidence **(Fig. 21)**. We believe that we have found the negative impressions of the walls of the Holy of Holies of Solomon's Temple and also the emplacement of the Ark of the Covenant (see below). These two discoveries have made a more accurate reconstruction possible.

One of the problems with making reconstruction drawings of Solomon's Temple is that the two descriptions of Solomon's Temple in the Hebrew Bible—the one in the First Book of Kings and the other in the Second Book of Chronicles—appear not to agree with each other.

According to the Hebrew Bible, the Books of Kings are considered to be part of the pre-exilic historical books called "The Early Prophets" and are thought to have been written by the prophet Jeremiah. The Books of Chronicles are part of a post-exilic work that includes also the Books of Ezra and Nehemiah. This conclusion is based on a similarity of style in these books and also on the fact that the last verses in Chronicles are identical to the first verses in the Book of Ezra.

It is therefore our premise that in the older First Book of Kings we have a description of the Temple as it was indeed built during the reign of King Solomon, while the Temple described in the Second Book of Chronicles appears to have been extensively reconstructed at a later date, probably during the reign of King Hezekiah (see below).

This two-Temple theory is not illogical. Even in modern times, hardly any building survives in its original state for four hundred years. We will look later at the evidence for structural damage to the Temple building in the record of its history (see below).

It will then become clear that two different temple buildings are described in the books of Kings and Chronicles, although the main inner core may have survived.

Solomon's Temple in the Book of Kings

The main description of Solomon's Temple is found in the Book of Kings[7]. Large amounts of stone and wood were necessary for its construction. Limestone is freely available in the Jerusalem mountains, but large cedar beams had to be imported from Lebanon. King Solomon therefore enlisted the help of Hiram, King of Tyre. Josephus refers to the correspondence between the two kings, letters that in his time were apparently still preserved in the archives of Tyre (*Ant.* 8.50–55).

According to Josephus, King Hiram was glad to have received a letter from King Solomon, to which he replied,

King Eiromos [Hiram] to King Solomon. It is proper to praise God for having given to you, who are a wise man endowed with every virtue, your father's royal power. As for me, I am very glad of this and I will assist you in all the things mentioned in your letter. I will have my men cut down many great cedars and cypresses and send them down to the sea, and will order my servants to put together a raft and sail and deliver them at whatever place in your country you may choose, and then your men shall carry them to Jerusalem. And take care, on your part, to furnish us in return for them with grain, of which we are in need because we live on an island (or peninsula).

The materials for the construction of the Tabernacle had come from Egypt and it is interesting to note that at least the wood for Solomon's Temple also originated in a foreign land.

The House of the LORD (*bayit Yahweh*)

From the Temple description in 1 Kings 6 and 7, it is obvious that

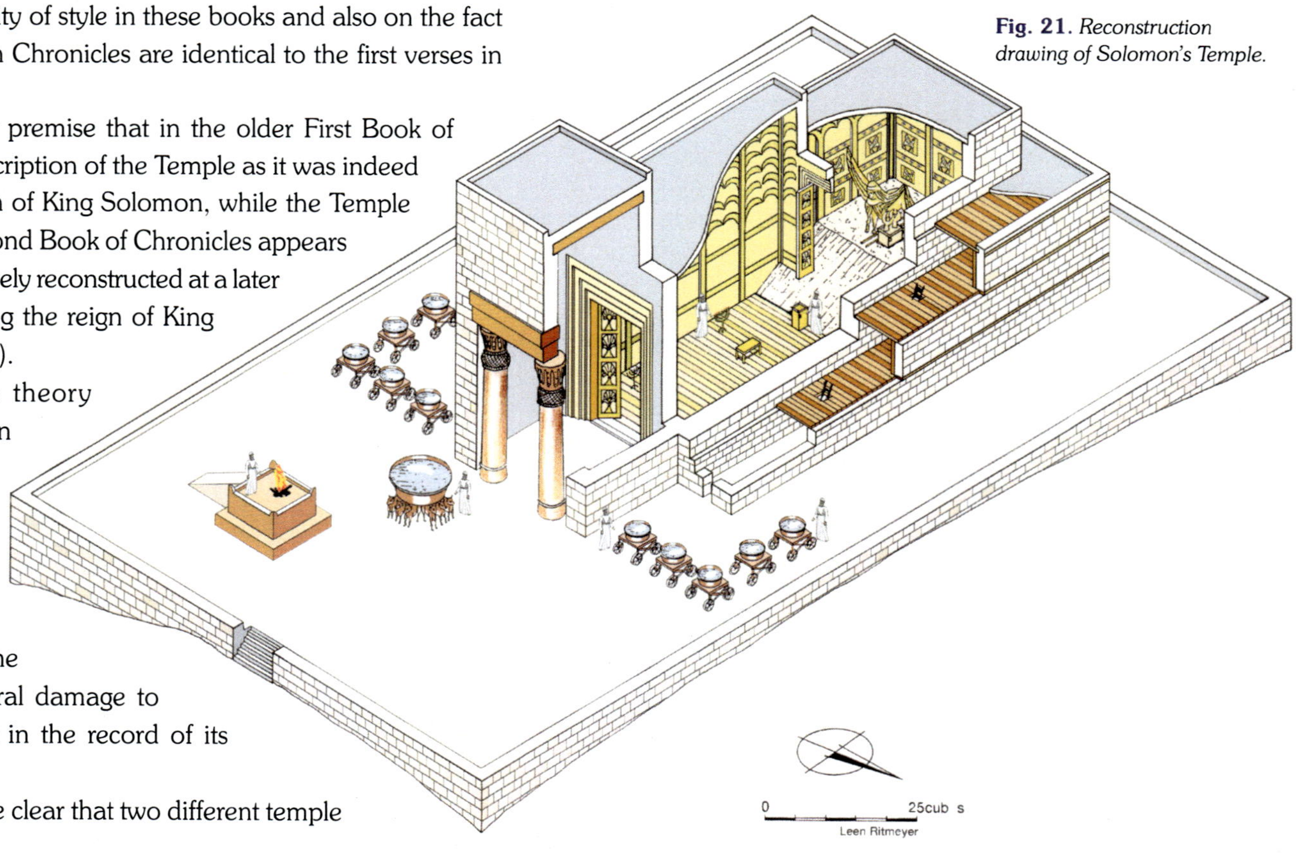

Fig. 21. *Reconstruction drawing of Solomon's Temple.*

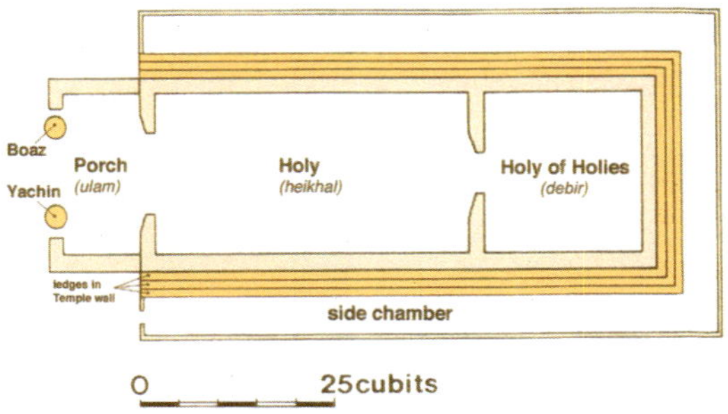

Fig. 22. *Plan and E-W section of Solomon's Temple.*

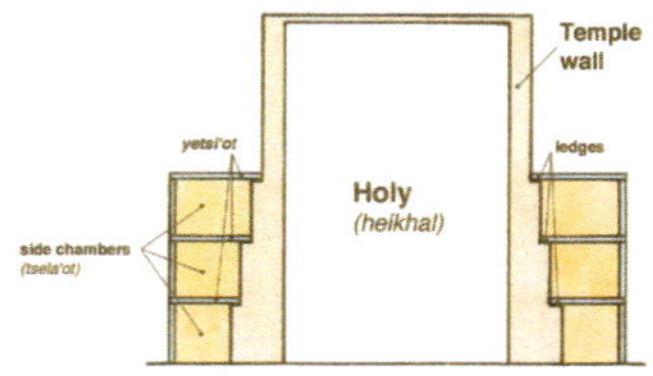

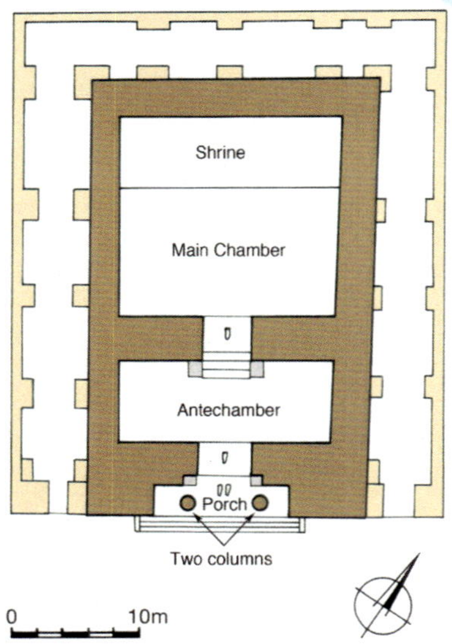

Fig. 23 *(right). Plan of the temple of Ein Dara. This temple is the earliest of the three, having existed from about 1300–740* B.C. *It is also the closest parallel to the Temple of Solomon as, in its later phase (900–740* B.C.*), a continuous corridor of side chambers were built on three sides of the building. This feature is strongly reminiscent of the side chambers,* tsela'ot, *that surrounded the Jerusalem Temple.*

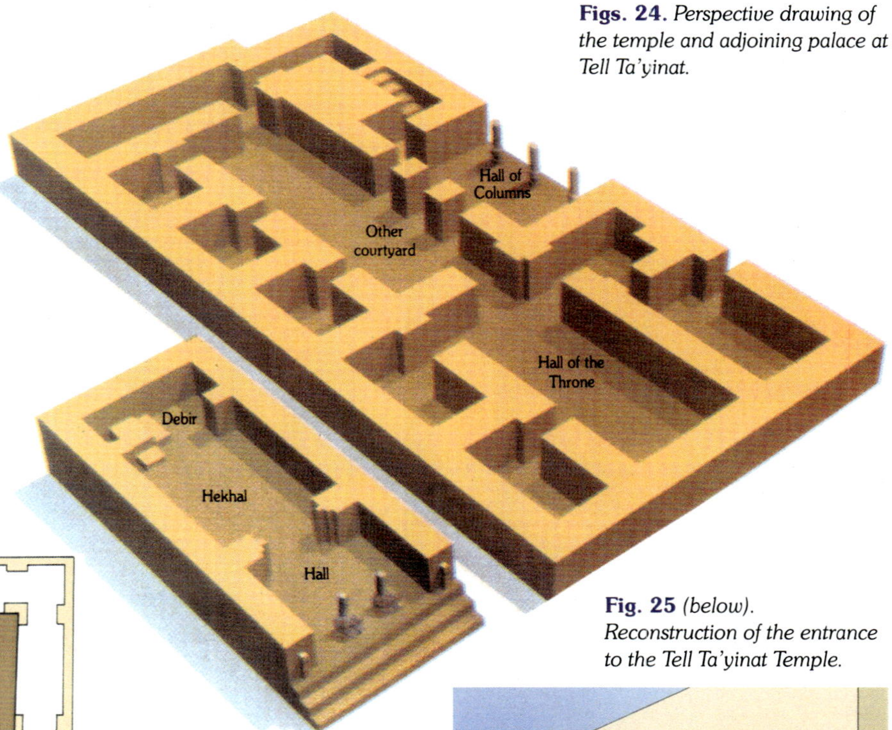

Figs. 24. *Perspective drawing of the temple and adjoining palace at Tell Ta'yinat.*

Fig. 25 *(below). Reconstruction of the entrance to the Tell Ta'yinat Temple.*

(above and right) The eighth century B.C. *construction date of the temple at Tell Ta'yinat means that it was built about 200 years after Solomon's Temple. The lions we see supporting the pillars of the portico were not a feature of the Jerusalem Temple. However, being part of an administrative complex, as was the Temple of Solomon, this temple casts light on the size of its adjoining palace in relation to the temple.*

the whole building was called "The House (*bayit*) of the LORD," although the building had three distinct subdivisions. Approaching the front of the building, which faced more or less east toward the highest peak of the Mount of Olives, one would first encounter the *ulam*, or Porch, then the *heikhal*, which is the first chamber of the *bayit*, also called the Holy, and lastly the inner chamber, which is referred to as the *debir*, or Holy of Holies.

The general dimensions of the *bayit* and the *ulam* are given in 1 Kings 6:2,3. These dimensions refer to the inner measurements, while the thickness of walls and other architectural elements, such as doors and partitions, are not given. The length of 60 cubits (103 ft. 2 in. or 31.50 m) excludes that of the *ulam*, which is 10 cubits (17 ft. 2 in. or 5.25 m) from east to west. The total inner dimensions, including the *ulam*, were 70 cubits (120 ft. 7 in. or 36.75 m) long, 20 cubits (34 ft. 5 in. or 10.50 m) wide and 30 cubits (51 ft. 7 in. or 15.75 m) high. Temples with a similar plan to that of Solomon's Temple have been found in Ein Dara and in Tell Ta'yinat in Syria. All three temples have two columns that supported the roof of a portico, a main hall and a shrine—the so-called "long-room plan." This layout is believed to have originated in Syria in the second millennium B.C. and then spread south **(see Figs. 22, 23, 24–25)**.

Verse 4 tells us that there were "windows of narrow lights" (*halonei shequfim 'atumim*) in the building **(Fig. 26)**. These openings were most likely restricted to the *heikhal*, where the priests needed light during their daily administrations. The Hebrew for window (*halon*) means an aperture, *shequfim* indicates that light could penetrate through the windows, while *'atumim* actually means that they could be closed. Usually, this is interpreted as windows that are narrow on the outside, to let the light in and keep the heat out, and broad on the inside, so as to maximize the amount of light that can enter the building. Windows of this type are well known in warmer climates. It is also possible that these windows could be closed with shutters, or that they had some kind of grille to let light in and keep animals such as rodents and birds out.

Fig. 26

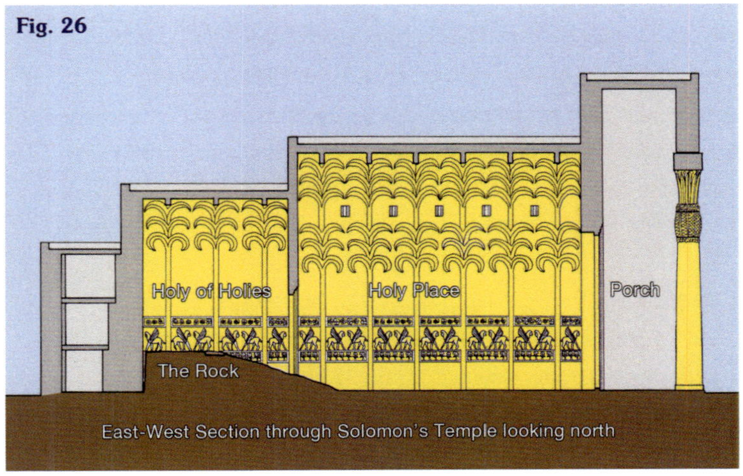

Fig. 27. *Reconstruction model of Solomon's Temple.*

The Roof and Walls of the House

The roof of the *bayit* was made of cedar wood (verse 10) with cross beams (*gebim*) running from wall to wall and boards (*sederot*) intersecting from beam to beam.

In verse 15, we read that the inner stone walls of the *bayit*, from ground to ceiling, were covered with boards of cedar wood and that the floor was made of planks of fir wood (cypress). According to verse 30, these planks were coated on both sides with gold. One might assume that the whole of the Temple had a wooden floor. However, the next verse, 16, which describes the *debir*, mentions only the wall boards and no planks for the floor. This would be in harmony with our finding of the emplacement of the Ark of the Covenant, which King Solomon had to prepare by cutting a horizontal basin in the rock (see 1 Kings 6:19; 8:6; 8:21, and later pp. 35, 36). It appears that only the *heikhal* had a wooden floor. It was made of fir, as were the doors leading into this chamber.

The Side Chambers

The *bayit* was surrounded by a wooden, three-story-high structure **(Fig. 27)**. The general name for this wooden encasement is the *yatsia*‘, which only occurs in the singular, and is made up of three *tsela'ot*. This latter term is derived from the Hebrew for ribs, while *yatsia*‘ means spreading out and is closely related to *yatsua*‘, which means a bed. The whole wooden construction therefore extended from the *bayit* and was built around it like a ribcage of three layers, each of which was five cubits high.

This structure, made from cedars, was built against the outer wall of the *bayit*, which had one-cubit-wide ledges on which the *tsela'ot* rested. To keep the outer wall of the *yatsia*‘ straight, we are told that the width of the bottom story was 5 cubits, the middle one 6 cubits and the one on top, 7 cubits. To prevent this construction from collapsing, a stone wall may have been built on the outside. The entrance at the right-hand side of the building and the three stories were connected by *lulim*, a term usually interpreted as trapdoors rather than winding staircases. Simple ladders would have been used to climb from floor to floor.

The Wall Construction

According to 1 Kings 6:7, the walls of the *bayit* were built of whole stones (*even shlema*) and no sound of hammer or axe or any other metal tool was heard whilst the *bayit* was built. According to some scholars the *bayit* was built with unhewn stones. However, the word "whole" can also mean "perfect." The fact that no iron tools were heard when the building was erected does not necessarily mean that no iron tools were used to cut the stones. It is more likely that the stones were dressed to perfection in the quarries, using the usual stonecutters' tools. Only after all the stones were beautifully squared were they transported to the building site, with no further need for iron tools. If an imperfect stone reached the construction site, it was probably rejected by the builders. King Herod the Great followed a similar procedure when he built the Second Temple many centuries later.

The Holy of Holies

The *debir* or *kodesh hakodashim* (Holy of Holies) itself is described in verses 19 to 32. It was a cube of 20 cubits, separated from the 30-cubit-high *heikhal* by a wooden partition made entirely of olive wood. There was no stone partition between the *debir* and the *heikhal*, so that the whole house was in essence one long chamber with doors facing east **(see Fig. 4)**. The walls of the inner sanctuary were covered with boards of cedar from the rocky ground up to the ceiling and decorated with cherubim, palm trees and open flowers, just like the rest of the walls and doors. The designs were carved in the cedar wood and then overlaid with gold leaf. From 1 Kings 8:12, which informs us that "*The Lord said that he would dwell in the thick darkness*," it may be deduced that the *debir* had no windows.

The problem with the height of the *debir* and the *heikhal* is the ten-cubit difference between the two. Some have suggested that there was a secret chamber above the *debir*, while others believe that it was built on a raised platform with steps leading up to it. Both proposals rest on the belief that the roof of the Temple building was level. However, this need not be so and this form of construction is certainly not mentioned in the sources. Our proposal puts the *debir* over the Rock (see below), which is about 5 cubits higher than the area to the east. Given that the *debir* was 20 cubits high, its roof must have stood 25 cubits above the floor level of the *heikhal*. The height of the *heikhal* was 30 cubits, and therefore the roof of the *debir* must have been 5 cubits[8] lower than the roof of the *heikhal*.

Two Large Cherubim

Inside the *debir* stood the two large cherubim made of olive wood and covered with gold **(Fig. 28)**. They were ten cubits high with a wingspan of ten cubits, and would thus touch the walls with their outer wing tips and one another's inner wing tips. We are not told what they looked like, only that they had wings. Josephus was not

Fig. 28 *(left). The two large cherubim.*

Fig. 29 *(right). Facade of Solomon's Temple.*

willing to speculate on the subject, writing in *Antiquities* 8.73, *"As for the cherubim themselves, no one can say or imagine what they looked like."*

The prophet Ezekiel, in his vision of the cherubim in chapters 1 and 10, described composite creatures that had four wings and four faces: namely those of a man, a lion, an ox and an eagle. Many ancient ivories have been found in Israel, Egypt, Phoenicia and Mesopotamia, portraying composite figures having a human head, a body (usually of a lion, but sometimes of an ox) and eagle's wings. Scholars usually refer to these representations as cherubim. As these are the only prototypes dating from about the time of the building of Solomon's Temple, we have applied elements of these figures in our portrayal of the large cherubim in the *debir*.

The Ark of the Covenant

These two cherubim were placed over the Ark of the Covenant, in which Moses had placed the two tablets of the Law. Later Aaron's rod that had budded was placed in it (Num. 17:10) together with the golden pot that held the manna (Ex. 16:33; Hebrews 9:4). In the Temple description of the First Book of Kings, however, we are told that the Ark contained only the tablets of stone (1 Kings 8:9).

The Doors of the Temple

Solomon's Temple had two sets of doors. The first set, made of fir, opened into the *heikhal*. Each door had two leaves and was decorated with carved figures of cherubim, palm trees and rosettes, overlaid with gold leaf **(Fig. 29)**.

In 1 Kings 6:33, we are told that the doorframe was made of olive wood, "of a fourth part." This latter phrase is difficult to understand. Does it mean that the door frame took up a fourth part of the width of the wall, which would make the door very small, or do we have here a description of a recessed door frame made of four stepped frames? This is the opinion of some scholars and we have incorporated this idea into our reconstruction. The door into the *debir* had five frames. The whole partition between the *heikhal* and the *debir* was made of olive wood, including the carved doors. There was no veil in Solomon's Temple. Of Israel's sanctuaries, only the Tabernacle and Herod's Temple contained veils.

The Two Pillars of Bronze

In the following chapter, 1 Kings 7, we read, in connection with the Porch, about the construction of the two pillars of bronze, which were 18 cubits (31 ft. or 9.45 m) high and had elaborate double capitals **(Fig. 30)**. The first capital, 5 cubits high, was apparently round in shape and surrounded by nets in which pomegranates were set. Above, another capital, 4 cubits high, had the appearance of a lily. The names of the pillars are *Yachin* ("He will establish") and *Boaz* ("in strength"), indicating that God himself is the one who will establish the Temple, just as he indicated to David in 2 Samuel 7:25:

> *And now, O LORD God, the word that thou hast spoken concerning thy servant, and concerning his house, establish it for ever, and do as thou hast said.*

The height of these columns was 18 cubits, although in 2 Chronicles 3:15 the height is given as 35 cubits. Later we will see that this is not a mistake, but a later development in the construction of the Temple. We are told that these columns and other bronze items were cast in clay ground in the Jordan Valley (1 Kings 7:46) under the supervision of a certain Hiram, who belonged to the tribe of Naphtali.

Usually these pillars are thought to have been freestanding, but I have always understood, as did Fritz[9], that they supported the lintel of the *ulam*. The height of this porch is not given. However, it must have been at least 30 cubits high, as the columns with the capitals already

Fig. 30. *Close-up view of the two bronze pillars.*

Fig. **31**. *The sanctuary walls of Megiddo.*

Fig. 32 *(below). Wall of the sanctuary at Tel Dan.*

Fig. 33. *Bronze basin, known as "the sea".*

Fig. 34. *The ten smaller basins set alongside "the sea".*

reached 27 cubits. A large lintel resting on the capitals must have been at least one cubit high and therefore the roof of the porch could have been level with the roof of the *heikhal*. From an architectural point of view, however, it would be more pleasing for the porch to be a little higher than the main building, more so since the roof of the *kodesh hakodashim* was lower than that of the Holy Place.

The Courtyard of the Temple

This sanctuary was set in a courtyard within walls constructed of successive layers of three courses of hewn stone and beams of cedar wood. Remains of such constructions have been found at Megiddo[10] **(Fig. 31)** and Tel Dan[11] **(Fig. 32)**. Recesses in the stones of the platform at Dan show that these beams were about 4 inches (10 cm) high and 8 inches (20 cm) wide. These wooden beams probably served to stabilize the stone coursing and to keep the courses horizontal.

Inside the Temple courtyard stood a great bronze basin, known, because of its size, as "the sea" **(Fig. 33)**. It rested on the hindquarters of twelve bronze oxen. Ten smaller basins, in two groups of five, were set on elaborate wheeled stands **(Fig. 34)**.

THE SERVICE OF THE TEMPLE

With the building of Solomon's Temple and based on its prior preparation by David, there appears to have been a shift away from a sacrificial emphasis to one that included praise through music.

One would have expected that all three main festivals that originated in the Tabernacle, the feasts of Passover and Unleavened Bread, the feast of Weeks and that of Tabernacles would have been kept. Indeed, it is recorded that Solomon, after the dedication of the Temple:

> *...offered burnt offerings unto the LORD on the altar of the LORD, which he had built before the porch, Even after a certain rate every day, offering according to the commandment of Moses, on the sabbaths, and on the new moons, and on the solemn feasts, three times in the year, even in the feast of unleavened bread, and in the feast of weeks, and in the feast of tabernacles. And he appointed, according to the order of David his father, the courses of the priests to their service, and the Levites to their charges, to praise and minister before the priests, as the duty of every day required: the porters also by their courses at every gate: for so had David the man of God commanded.* (2 Chron. 8:12–14)

And every day the morning and evening sacrifices would have been offered on the Altar of Burnt Sacrifices, according to the Mosaic injunction (Ex. 29:38–42), while inside, in the Holy Place, incense was offered and the lamps of the Lampstand were trimmed and lit again at the same times (Ex. 30:7–9). Every Sabbath, the shewbread was replaced with fresh bread. This latter ceremony is attested in David's time when he came to the priest Ahimelech in Nob and asked for food (1 Sam. 21:1–6).

However, there are very few references in the Hebrew Bible to indicate that the three main feasts were kept. King Hezekiah found when he wanted the nation to keep the Passover, that the people had not prepared themselves. They had not kept this feast officially "for a long time" and therefore had to keep it in the second month (2 Chron. 30:1–5). And two generations later, it was still not being kept properly. In the beginning of the reign of Josiah, the young king found that the feast was observed after a sort, but in the high places and not in Jerusalem (2 Kings 23:9). Sweeping religious reforms were needed before it could be recorded of Josiah's Passover, in 2 Kings 23:22, that such a celebration of the feast had not been held "from the days that the Judges that judged Israel, nor in all the days of the kings of Israel, nor of the kings of Judah."

There is only one reference to the Feast of Weeks in 2 Kings 4:42. In the time of Elisha, we are told that a man from Baal-shalisha brought "twenty loaves of barley," which were the "bread of the firstfruits."

Solomon's Temple was dedicated in the seventh month and they kept "the feast" (which must have the Feast of Tabernacles, 1 Kings 8:65; 2 Chron. 7:8–10) for seven days. There are no further references to the three main festivals until the Post-Exilic period.

From Tabernacle to Temple

One of the reasons why these feasts were not kept regularly at this time may have been the separation of the Ark from the Tabernacle (with the latter now in Gibeon and the Ark in Jerusalem) and the eventual building of the Temple.

David had not only collected many materials for the temple, but he also changed the service. The regular services continued in the Tabernacle, but a new service of music and praise, based on the Psalms of David, was introduced in front of the Ark in Jerusalem, which continued after Solomon actually built the Temple.

SOLOMON'S TEMPLE IN THE SECOND BOOK OF CHRONICLES

So far, our description of Solomon's Temple is based solely on the record of 1 Kings 6 and 7. Let us now examine the differences between this description and the one contained in 2 Chronicles 3 and 4. The reason for these differences is that the original Solomonic Temple suffered many years of destruction, deterioration and neglect. Five years after Solomon's death, in about 920 B.C., Shishak of Egypt ransacked the Temple and stripped it of its outer golden covering. Erosion would have set in and slowly weakened the outer walls. The Temple was again looted during the reign of Athaliah, daughter of a king of Israel and wife of King Jehoram of Judah. After the death of her son Ahaziah, she seized the throne in Jerusalem. Joash, the only royal heir to survive her murderous purge, sought donations from all the people of Judah to repair the damage. A massive earthquake that occurred in the last year of King Uzziah's reign again destroyed parts of the Temple. The three-storied construction and the Porch suffered heavy damage and King Ahaz caused further destruction by smashing all the bronze implements of the Temple, including the lavers and the two massive columns that supported the Porch. Ahaz then closed the doors of the Temple. Much more damage than is actually recorded in the biblical sources must have occurred during the reign of Ahaz, as witnessed by the record of the repair work which his son Hezekiah carried out to make the Temple functional again.

Hezekiah's Temple

When Hezekiah (c. 725–697 B.C. as sole ruler, and until his death in 686 B.C. with Manasseh as co-regent) began to reign after the death of his father Ahaz, his first act was the re-opening of the Temple doors (2 Chron. 29). To do so he first had to repair and strengthen the doors that must have been badly damaged. The priests and Levites then cleared the Temple of all the accumulated filth. The fact that a large number of priests labored for a week to cleanse the Temple shows how much rubbish had accumulated, not only in the *heikhal* but also in the *debir*. The rubbish removed by the Levites was dumped in the Kedron Valley. Vessels and furniture that had been dismantled or removed by Ahaz were collected or replaced.

Thus the Temple was rededicated and the services restored. Hezekiah then invited all Israel to come to Jerusalem to keep the feast of Passover. According to 2 Kings 18:4, Hezekiah also removed the high places, broke the standing stones, cut down the images of Asherah and broke the bronze serpent Moses had made, in order to stop the people from making it an object of idol worship.

Initially, Hezekiah appears to have repaired the Temple in haste, so as to make it serviceable again as quickly as possible. This may, however, have been a mere rescue operation, as we read in 2 Kings 18, that in the fourteenth year of Hezekiah's reign, Sennacherib came to Judah and captured many of its cities.

In order to prevent an attack on Jerusalem, Hezekiah paid Sennacherib a ransom, as recorded in verse 16:

> *At that time did Hezekiah cut off the gold from the doors of the Temple of the LORD, and from the pillars which Hezekiah king of Judah had overlaid, and gave it to the king of Assyria.*

The English text reads as though Hezekiah took off the gold from the two famous bronze pillars, Yachin and Boaz, which King Solomon had made. However, in the Hebrew text, the normal word for pillars, *amudim*, is not used but rather *umnot*, which means pilasters (rectangular columns projecting slightly from a wall such as found in the outer walls of the later Tomb of the Patriarchs in Hebron).

It is possible that by this time the two Solomonic pillars, each 18 cubits high, no longer existed. Hezekiah initially may have replaced the original pillars with simple pilasters on either side of the main entrance and overlaid them with gold. It is also an indication that Ahaz, when removing the two bronze pillars, must have also destroyed the Porch that the pillars supported.

However, the Temple description in 2 Chronicles 3:15 shows that two pillars, 35 cubits high, were made for the edifice. It is possible that Hezekiah restored the Temple after the Assyrian army was destroyed at Lachish. Some scholars believe that the events recorded in 2 Kings 18:17 refer to a second and later invasion[12]. If this was the case, Hezekiah could have rebuilt the Temple in the interlude, at a time when he was also strengthening the walls of Jerusalem. In any event, we believe that the two descriptions of Solomon's Temple differ sufficiently from one another to warrant the suggestion that two different buildings are described. The main core of the later building may still have had original elements from the first building.

Comparing the two accounts of the building of the Temple, the first in 1 Kings, chapters 6 and 7, and the second in 2 Chronicles, chapters 3 and 4, many other differences, apart from the height of the pillars, become apparent. The height of the first porch was not given; the second one was 120 cubits high. As the porch was probably proportionate in size to the pillars, one may assume that the first porch was lower than the second. In the first account, the Temple is surrounded by three stories of chambers; in the second account these chambers are replaced by upper chambers. The first laver had knobs under the rim; the second had two rows of oxen. The first contained 2,000 baths (12,000 gallons, 44,000 liters) and the second 3,000 (18,000 gallons, 66,000 liters).

From the differences between the two records, we must conclude that the Temple destroyed by the Babylonians was not the same as that constructed by Solomon. During the First Temple period, which lasted more than four hundred years, the Temple had undergone the many changes and repairs that we have mentioned. This then, we believe, is the reason for the two differing descriptions: Solomon's Temple had obviously suffered so much from neglect, destruction and earthquakes that King Hezekiah had it completely renovated.

Differences in Temple descriptions	1 Kings 6–7	2 Chronicles 3–4
Internal dimensions (*cubits*)	6.2. L×W×H = 60×20×30	3.3. L×W = 60×20
Porch (*ulam*)	6.3. 20 broad, 10 wide	3.4. 20 broad, 120 high
Chambers	6.5,6. 3 side stories high	3.9. upper chambers
Shewbread table	7.48. one table	4.8. 10 tables
Partition between *heikhal* and *debir*	6.31. doors of olive wood	3.14. veil
Holy of Holies	6.20. 20×20×20	3.8. 20×20
2 Pillars of bronze	7.15. 18 high; circumference 12	3.15. 35 high
Capitals	7.16. lower capital, 5 high 7.17. 7 nets 7.19. upper capital, 4 high	3.15. one capital, 5 high with chains
Laver	7.23. 10 diameter; 5 high; 30 circumference 7.26. 2,000 baths decoration of lilies	4.2. 10 diameter; 5 high; 30 circumference 4.5. 3,000 baths decoration of oxen

This was the Temple that the Babylonians destroyed. However, despite all the alterations and building activities, this last Temple is still referred to as the First Temple. The one built after the Babylonian Exile was called the Second Temple. The differences between the two buildings are tabulated above (measurements in cubits).

Hezekiah also built chambers (*lesachot*) on the Temple Mount (2 Chron. 31:11). These were initially built as storerooms for the tithes. Later we read that some of these rooms (or additional ones) were used by scribes. Thus we read of the *"chamber of the sons of Hanan, the son of Igdaliah, a man of God, which was by the chamber of the princes, which was above the chamber of Maaseiah the son of Shallum, the keeper of the door"* (Jer. 35:4); *"the chamber of Gemariah the son of Shaphan the scribe, in the higher court, at the entry of the new gate of the LORD's house"* (Jer 36:10); and the chamber of Elishama the scribe (Jer. 36:12, 20).

Similar chambers are mentioned in the books of Ezra and Nehemiah, indicating that these chambers were rebuilt after the Babylonian Exile.

Hezekiah's Square Temple Mount

As will be explained below, it is possible to suggest that King Hezekiah, after having rebuilt the Temple, created a 500-cubit-square artificial mount around the Temple in order to enhance the glory of the sacred complex **(Fig. 35).** This measurement of 500 cubits is based on a reference in the Mishnaic tractate *Middot*. The size of the Temple Mount (Hebrew, *har habbayit*), is given in *Middot* 2:1: *"The Temple Mount measured five hundred cubits by five hundred cubits."*

Despite the fact that the Mishnah, including *Middot*, was compiled some time after the Roman destruction of the Temple in Jerusalem (probably during the second century A.D.), this measurement of 500 cubits was found to be correct for the sides of the square pre-Hasmonean Temple Mount. The fact that Herod's outer enclosures are not mentioned at all indicates that *Middot* refers only to the area occupied by the Temple Mount as it existed at the end of the First Temple period. Only this original, square "Mountain of the House" seems to have been "holy" according to the author(s) of *Middot*. The building activities of Herod around this square entity were simply ignored.

The Second Book of Chronicles 33:15 may indicate that this artificially created Temple Mount already existed in the time of Manasseh, when the Temple Mount is referred to as *har bayit-Yahweh*. Manasseh was an idol worshipper and therefore unlikely to have improved the Temple Mount. Thus, it is most likely that it was his father, Hezekiah, who actually constructed this mount that surrounded the Temple. The prophets Isaiah (2:2) and Micah (4:1), who lived during the time of Hezekiah, looked forward to a glorious future for the Temple Mount, as it says in Isaiah:

> *...and it shall come to pass in the last days, that* har bayit-Yahweh *shall be established in the top of the mountains, and shall be exalted above the hills; and all nations shall flow unto it.*

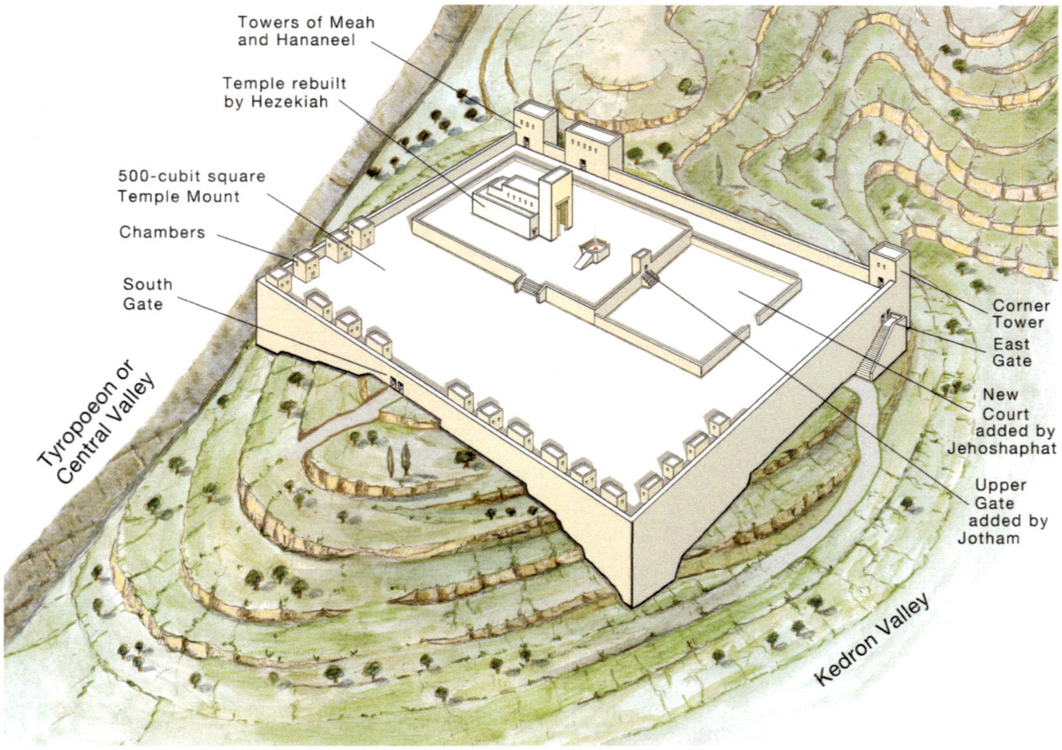

Fig. 35. *The Temple Mount in the time of Hezekiah.*

It is generally understood that Solomon built his palaces to the immediate south of the Temple. It would be logical to assume that the construction of a large 500-cubit-square Temple Mount would have obliterated these palaces. But as Mazar[13] pointed out, only two palaces are mentioned as having been destroyed in 586 B.C. The first to be destroyed was the relatively new palace near the Middle Gate on the Western Hill of Jerusalem and one month later the old palace in the City of David (2 Kings 25:9–10). There is no mention of the destruction of Solomon's palace adjacent to the Temple. It is possible that Solomon's palace complex had fallen into disrepair by the time of Hezekiah and was removed in order to build the new Temple Mount.

The influx of people settling in Jerusalem after the Assyrian invasion had already caused Hezekiah to encompass the Western Hill with a city wall[14]. Excavations in the City of David have also shown that this area was enclosed by the new city wall built by Hezekiah. He may therefore also have felt the need to enlarge the then existing Temple Mount to accommodate the larger number of new worshippers.

As mentioned earlier, this enlargement of the Solomonic Temple court would have necessitated demolishing the palatial complex that Solomon had built to the immediate south of the Temple, and which, according to 1 Kings 7:1–8, included Solomon's House with its court, the Hall of Pillars, the Throne Hall and the House of the Forest of Lebanon **(Fig. 36).** The dismantling of this latter building may have been alluded to by the prophet Isaiah:

Fig. 36. *The Solomonic complex.*

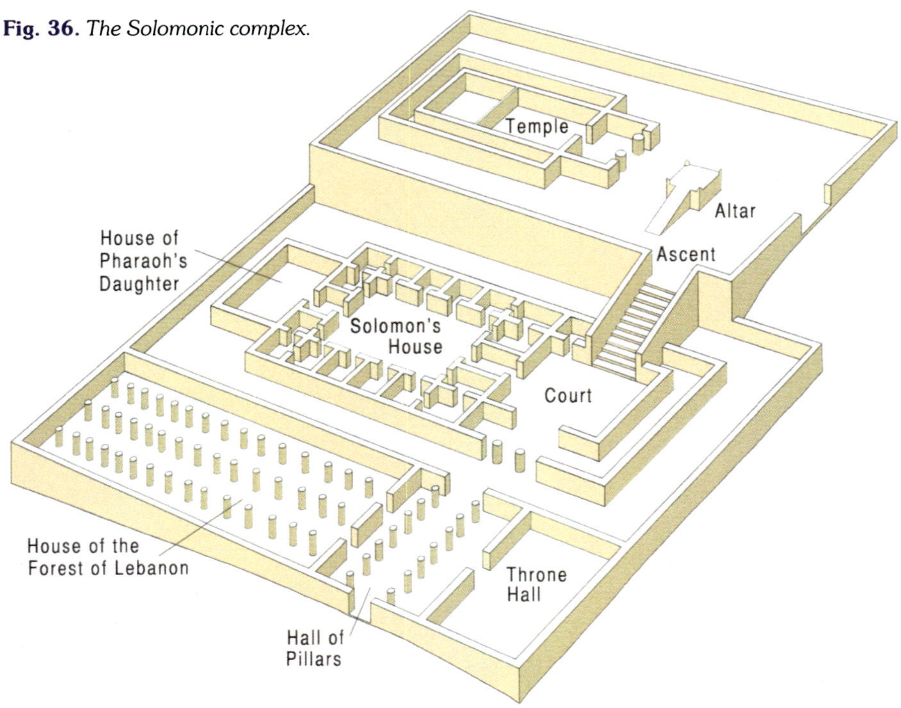

> *And he discovered the covering of Judah, and thou didst look in that day to the armour of the house of the forest.* (Isa. 22:8)

The "Covering (*masach*) of Judah" may have referred to a covered royal ascent from Solomon's Palace to the Temple. As Isaiah was referring to activities in the time of King Hezekiah, this further strengthens our proposal that it was he who built a new square Temple Mount around Solomon's Temple.

The Temple Mount was referred to as a citadel, called the *birah*, at the end of the First Temple and beginning of the Second Temple periods. The reference in the Bible is 1 Chronicles 29:1–2,19:

> *Furthermore David the king said unto all the congregation, Solomon my son, whom alone God hath chosen, is yet young and tender, and the work is great for the palace* (birah)[15] *is not for man, but for the Lord God. Now I have prepared with all my might for the House of my God the gold for the things of gold....*

(Then David asks God to) give unto Solomon a perfect heart, to keep thy commandments, thy testimonies, and thy statutes, and to do all these things, and to build the palace (birah), *for the which I have made provision.*

As the Book of Chronicles was written after the exile, it is evident that the square Temple Mount was already in existence at the time of writing. The reference to a Solomonic *birah* is anachronistic, as the Chronicler would have been familiar only with the Temple Mount as it existed at the end of the First Temple period.

The Discovery of the Archaeological Remains of the 500-cubit-square Temple Mount

The author has been able to identify archaeological remains on the present-day Temple Mount that have confirmed these conclusions[16] **(Fig. 37)**.

In 19 B.C., Herod the Great began to build his mighty Temple Mount, doubling the size of the earlier platform, so that this square *har habbayit* became a court surrounded by newly added areas in the north, west and south. Nevertheless, this square court was still referred to as "The Temple Mount," as it was the sacred precinct of the First Temple period.

On the Temple Mount today, two main levels can be discerned. Most of the present-day interior level of the Temple Mount is a more or less flat surface, although it slopes down a little from north to south. The Dome of the Rock, however, stands on an elevated or raised platform that can be reached by eight different stairways.

The research began at the stairway that leads up to the platform of the Dome of the Rock at its northwest corner **(Fig. 38)**. We have shown that the 17-meter- (56-ft.-) long bottom step (the *step*) is the remains of a massive ancient wall, the ashlars of which have margins and roughly hewn bosses[17]. As the *step* is located 500 cubits from the Eastern Wall of the Temple Mount, we have suggested that this *step* is the remains of the Western Wall of the Mishnaic Temple Mount. There is another ashlar to the immediate east of the northernmost stone of this *step*. The northern edges of both these stones are located exactly on the line of the northern boundary of the raised platform. The northern boundary of the raised platform is built, according to Warren, on a squared-off rock scarp. We have therefore suggested that this northern rock scarp formed the foundation for the northern boundary wall of the square mount and that the northernmost ashlar of the *step* forms the northwest corner of the 500-cubit-square Temple Mount.

A major feature of the Eastern Wall of this 500-cubit-square Temple Mount is the well-known Golden Gate, now blocked on the outside. The Golden Gate was built during the Umayyad period, when the Temple Mount was restored as a center for Muslim worship[18]. This was also when the Dome of the Rock and al-Aqsa mosque were built, at the end of the seventh century. To both Jews and Arabs, this gate is known as the Gate of Mercy (Hebrew: *sha'ar ha-rachamim*).

In the 1970s, the author carried out a complete architectural survey of the interior of the Golden Gate. The roof structure is made up of six domes, supported by two centrally placed columns, gateposts and sidewalls. Each of the sidewalls is decorated with four pilasters, topped by a decorative entablature. The most interesting

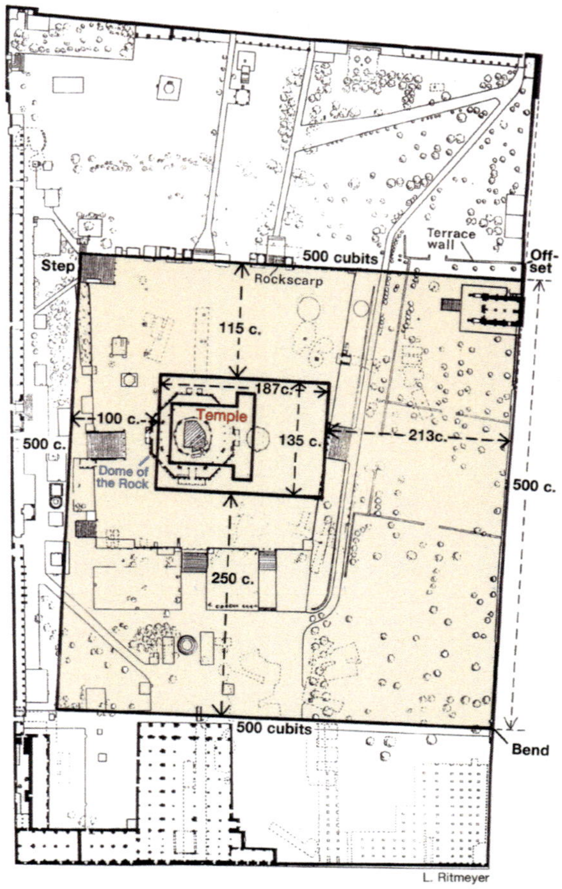

Fig. 37. *Plan of the Temple Mount today with indications of the 500-cubit-square Temple platform.*

Fig. 38. *The* step, *at the bottom of the stairway leading to the Dome of the Rock.*

features, however, are two massive monolithic gateposts at the east end of the side walls, the northern one being 15 feet (4.5 m) high, while the southern one stands at 12 feet (3.5 m) high[19]. They appear to be earlier than the Umayyad gateway, as the top of the gateposts don't line up with the interior masonry courses of this gate. This means that when the Golden Gate was built, it incorporated the surviving gateposts of an earlier gate into its structure **(Fig. 39)**. I have proposed that this earlier gate is most likely the Shushan Gate, mentioned in Mishnah *Middot* 1.3 as the only gate in the Eastern Wall. The gate was most probably given this name by builders who had returned from exile in Babylon and in whose memories the palace of Shushan lived on.

In the central section of the Eastern Wall of the Temple Mount, on either side of the Golden Gate, massive ashlars can be seen near the present ground level. The southern section, which is better preserved, is 51 feet (15.5 m) long **(Fig. 40)**, while that to the north is 68 feet (20.7 m) long **(Fig. 41)**. We had expected to see the northeast corner of the 500-cubit-square mount at a distance of 29 feet (8.84 m) north of the Golden Gate, in line with the northern boundary of the raised platform, but it could not be detected. Instead, this northern section continues north of the projected northeast corner of the square mount for another 39 feet (11.98 m). This part of the wall may have belonged to an integrated tower at the northeast corner. The corner of this tower appears as an *offset*[20] in the Eastern Wall of the present-day Temple Mount. We have concluded therefore that the 500-cubit-square Temple Mount refers to the platform only, excluding any towers that were built along its northern boundary.

In both these masonry sections, the ashlars, all of which have very rough and bulging bosses, are laid in header-stretcher fashion. It is reasonable to suggest that this visible masonry continues down to bedrock, which, at the northernmost point of the square Temple Mount, would then have been preserved to a height of 18 courses (59 ft. or 18 m)[21].

The ancient gateposts inside the Golden Gate are set on the same line as the Eastern Wall of the Temple Mount and line up with the massive masonry that can be seen on either side of the Golden Gate. These gateposts and the two masonry sections appear therefore to

Fig. 39

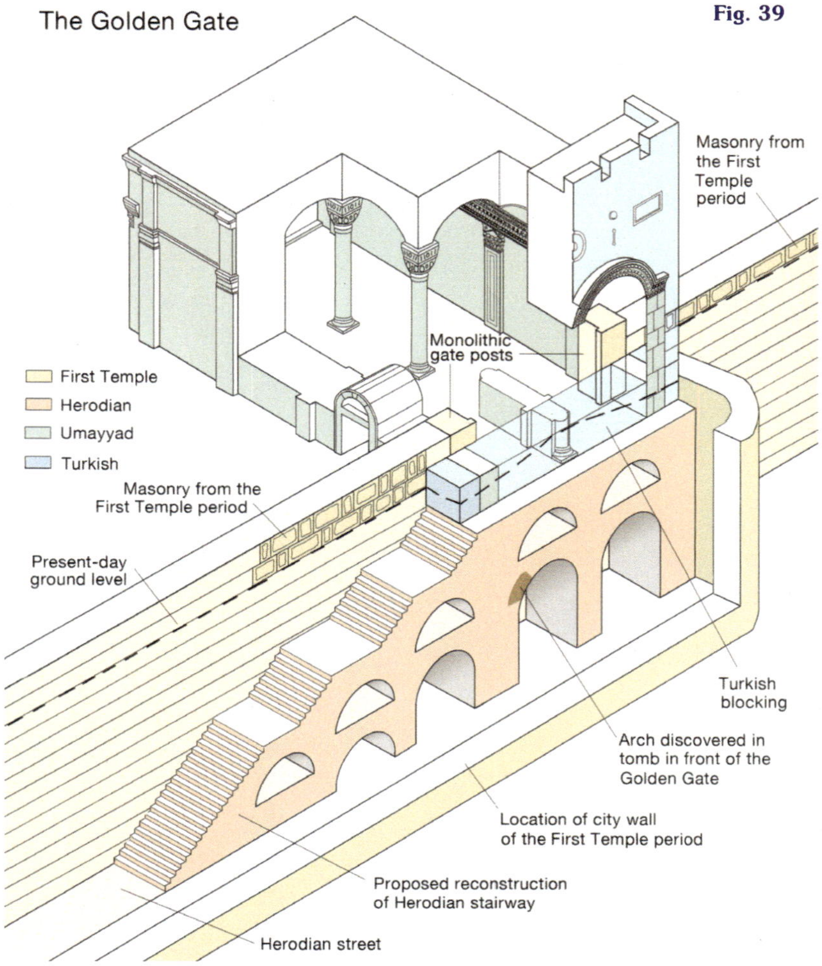

Fig. 40. *Ashlars south of the Golden Gate.*

Fig. 41. *Ashlars north of the Golden Gate.*

Fig. 42. *Elevation of early masonry visible on either side of the Golden Gate and (below) a proposed reconstruction of the Eastern Gate of the 500-cubit-square Temple Mount.*

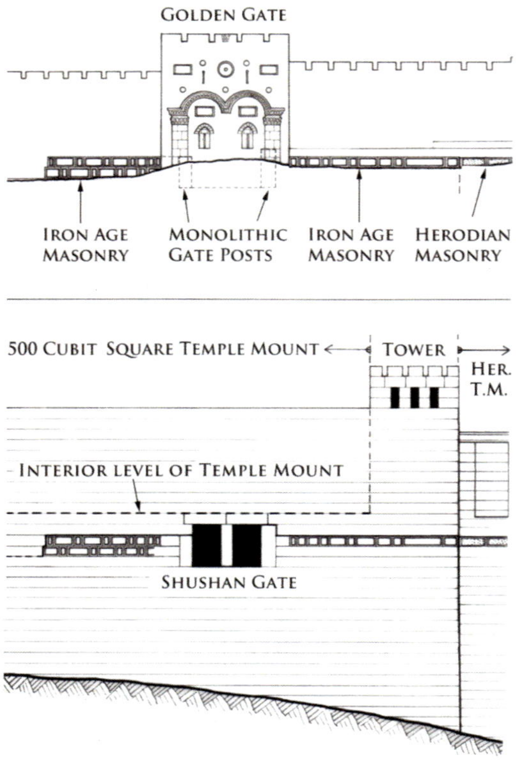

be part of the same construction. The top of the southern gatepost is level with the top of the ancient masonry that can be seen south of the Golden Gate. The northern gatepost is one stone course higher and is located only one stone course below the surface of the Temple Mount **(see Fig. 42)**. This means that the top of the original lintel would have been virtually level with the present-day level of the Temple Mount. This is the same level as that of the *step*, the remains of the Western Wall of the square Temple Mount, located at the foot of the northwest stairway that leads up to the raised platform of the Dome of the Rock.

In 2007, similar ashlars were identified approximately 13 feet (4 m) north of the projected southeast corner of the square Temple Mount[22]. Following this discovery, a close re-examination of Warren's "Elevation of the East Wall of the Noble Sanctuary"[23] showed that he had already noted these large ashlars. Today, at least five ashlars can be observed *in situ*, arranged in two courses **(Fig. 43)**. The top of these ashlars is located at 55 feet (17m) above bedrock, according to the levels given in the above-mentioned drawing by

Fig. 43. *Ashlars found* in situ *north of the conjectured southeast corner of the square Temple Mount.*

Fig. 44. *The Eastern Wall of the Temple Mount.*

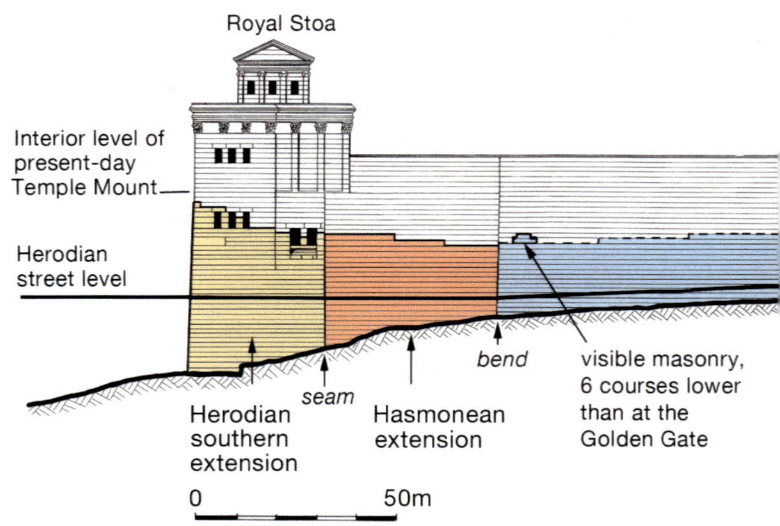

Warren. The nearby southeast corner, which because of its proximity to the preserved ashlars must still exist, is located at a point where the Eastern Wall bends a little. There is a protruding pillar high in the wall above, the so-called Pillar of Muhammad. We have called this point, where the wall changes direction slightly, the *bend*[24]. Assuming an average height of 1 m for the stone courses, the height of the southeast corner of the square Temple Mount has therefore been preserved to a height of 17 courses! The top of this section of masonry is located six courses lower than the masonry near the Golden Gate, or seven courses below the highest gatepost inside this gate **(Fig. 44)**. This means that the top of this section of masonry near the southeast corner is located only eight courses below the interior level of the present-day Temple Mount. It is legitimate to reconstruct the walls of the square Temple Mount to its highest preserved level. Measuring down from the level of the present-day Temple Mount, the southeast corner of the square Temple Mount would originally have stood 25 stone courses high. It is not known how much higher the original walls were, but it is reasonable to suggest that the square mount was surrounded by a parapet wall of at least 9 feet 10 inches (3 m) high. The minimum total height of this corner would therefore have been 92 feet (28 m).

As we will see below, it can be suggested that the northwest corner of the Hasmonean extension has been preserved to a great height also. As this corner is built against the southwest corner of the square Temple Mount, it can be reasoned that the southwest corner of the square Temple Mount has been preserved to a considerable height too. If this is indeed the case, then all four corners of the square Temple Mount have been preserved, the *step* at the northwest, the tower at the northeast, the southeast corner near the newly discovered stones at the *bend* and the southwest corner at the western Hasmonean extension wall **(Fig. 45)**.

The preserved remains of the Herodian Eastern Wall of the Temple Mount are highest at the northeast and southeast corners. That is because very large stones were used in the corner constructions, which the Romans in A.D. 70 must have found too heavy to shift. At the southeast corner, Herodian masonry is visible quite high above ground level and north of it Hasmonean masonry can be seen. To the north of the "straight joint" or *seam* **(Fig. 46)**,

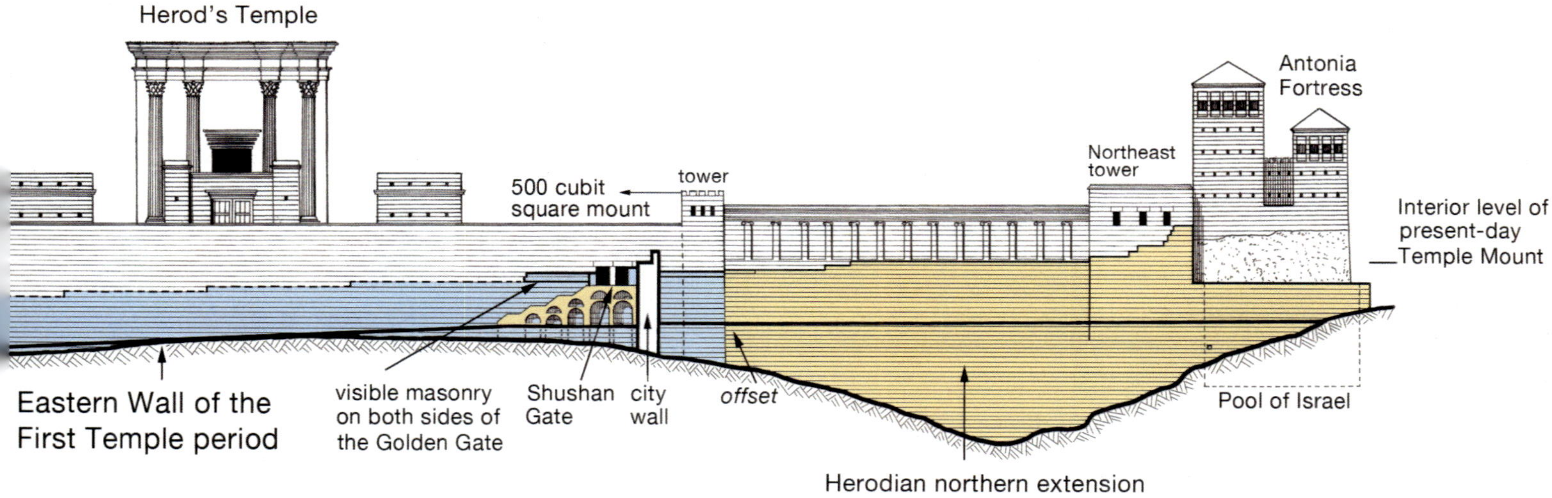

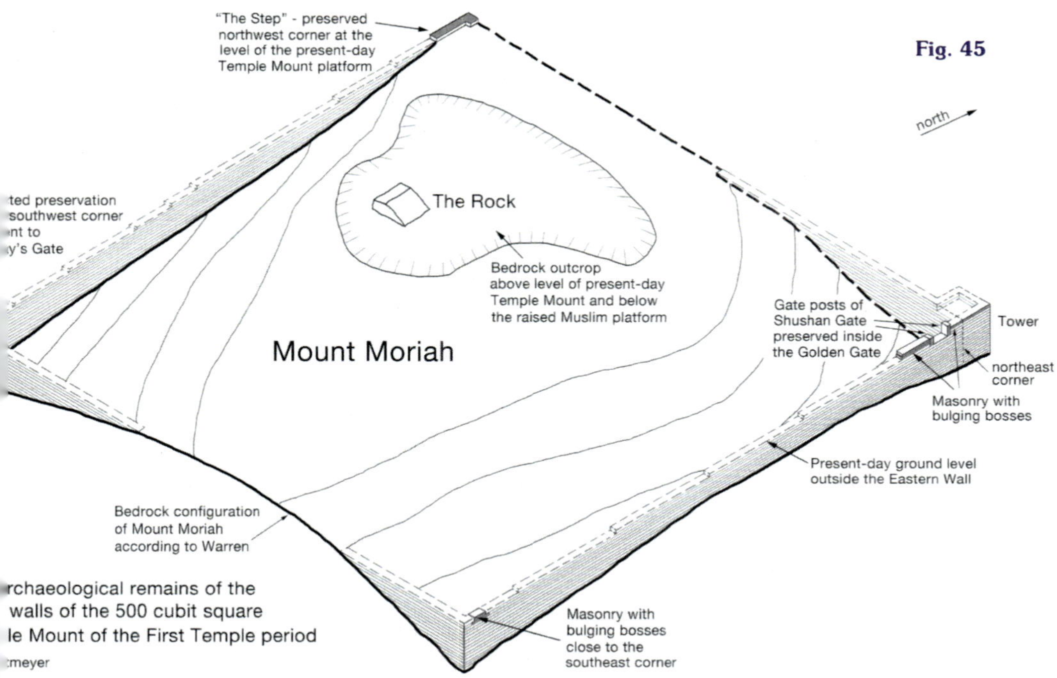

Fig. 45

Dating the Early Masonry in the Eastern Wall of the Temple Mount

In order to establish a historical date for this ancient masonry of the Eastern Wall, we have been looking for parallel constructions, as excavation is out of the question. One excellent example was found not too far away. In the 1860s, Warren, while tunnelling underground, discovered a large tower, which he called the "Extra Tower," some 300 feet (100 m) to the southwest of the southeast corner of the Temple Mount and south of the Triple Gate [26] **(Fig. 47)**. The area in which this early tower can be seen had been excavated by Dame Kathleen Kenyon in the 1960s. She called this area SII. This area

some 10 Hasmonean stone courses can be observed above ground level today.

As mentioned above, the ancient masonry near the Golden Gate can be seen one or two courses above ground level, i.e., above the level of the Muslim cemetery. The same is the case with the newly discovered ashlars near Muhammad's Pillar. It therefore appears reasonable to suggest that the central section of the Eastern Wall has been preserved more or less up to the present ground level on the outside. A line drawn from the top of the preserved courses south of the Golden Gate to the top of the preserved Hasmonean masonry would therefore give a general idea of the preservation of the Eastern Wall **(see Fig. 44)**. The newly discovered ashlars are therefore not an isolated piece of masonry, but part of the remaining Eastern Wall of the Square Temple Mount of the First Temple Period.

Building activities on such a scale here should not surprise us, as similar towering structures were built not much later, e.g., the unfinished great stone platform of Tall-i Takht Citadel, or Throne Hill (6th cent. B.C.) at Pasargadae and other ashlar terraces at Persepolis. Similar platform constructions can also be seen, for example, in the Temple of Eshmun near Sidon[25].

Fig. 46. *The "seam" near the southern end of the Eastern Wall.*

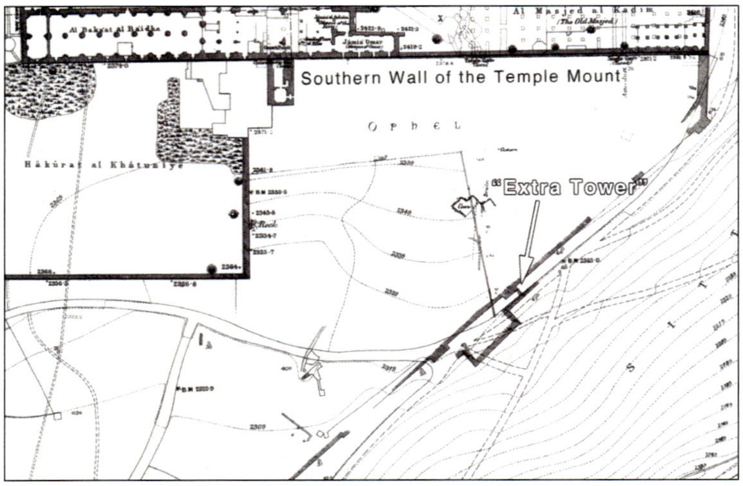

Fig. 47. *Warren's plan showing the "Extra Tower."*

was excavated in the 1970s by the team of the late Prof. Benjamin Mazar, during which time the author was working as archaeological architect for the Temple Mount Excavations. The excavation area was subsequently enlarged by Eilat Mazar. A Byzantine city wall was exposed, with a tower built into the wall. This tower was built, in turn, over the remains of an earlier tower **(Fig. 48)**. The stones of this latter tower, which appear rather weathered, still show some margins and rough, bulging bosses. Not only are the bosses very

Fig. 48 *(above). Byzantine tower built over the earlier, or "Extra Tower."*

Fig. 49 *(below). Header-and-stretcher construction of the "Extra Tower."*

similar to those of the ancient masonry near the Golden Gate, but so too is the header-and-stretcher construction **(Fig. 49)**.

The following are the comments made respectively by Warren, Kenyon, and more recently E. Mazar, about this particular masonry:

> *The masonry in the corner turret of the great tower consists of large drafted stones, 2 ft. to 3 ft. high, and 4 ft. to 8 ft. long, with roughly hewn bosses.*[27]
>
> *Beneath...the Byzantine wall...is a wall which probably belonged to a projecting tower. The date of these earliest walls, on the basis of the deposits against them, is...8th c.* BCE *or earlier. ...these walls were constructed...with irregular projecting bosses having margins on one, two or three sides.*[28]
>
> *...the Extra Tower could have been built in the 8th c....*[29]

As this masonry is identical to the ancient masonry on either side of the Golden Gate, its date may therefore have a bearing on that of the ancient masonry in the central section of the Eastern Wall of the Temple Mount. Masonry of this type is also known from other parts of the country. At Tel Dan and Samaria, for instance, walls with similar masonry of the First Temple period have been excavated, with ashlars having margins and rough bosses, laid in header and stretcher construction.

It would appear therefore that the early masonry in the Eastern Wall of the Temple Mount should be dated to the eighth century B.C. Historically this would fit very well. It was in the eighth century B.C. that Hezekiah ruled as King of Judah. During his reign, major building activities took place. The city of Jerusalem was expanded to include the southwest hill, which was encircled by a massive city wall. The late Prof. Nahman Avigad[30] excavated the central section of the northern part of this wall, which he identified as the Broad Wall mentioned in the Book of Nehemiah (Neh. 3:8; 12:38). As mentioned earlier, there was undoubtedly a need for a larger Temple court to accommodate the many new worshippers who had fled the Assyrian invasion and had settled in Jerusalem.

The Location of the Temple

Having established the location of the 500-cubit-square Temple Mount, the next step that needs to be taken is to find the location of the Temple itself. We need to jump forward in time to the Herodian period to be able to make use of some relevant historical information.

According to *Middot* 2:6 and 5:1, the Herodian Temple was located inside the Temple Court, which measured 187 by 135 cubits. The Temple (100×100×100 cubits) was placed symmetrically within the court, which included an 11-cubit-wide Court of the Israelites and a similar-sized Court of the Priests.

Behind the Temple, at the western end of the court, there was a space of 11 cubits and therefore the location of the Temple inside its court can be determined accurately on the Temple Mount. Although this in itself does not help determine the location of the Temple, *Middot* contains information about the dimensions of the courtyards surrounding the Temple Court. Once we determine the location of this inner court, then we can place the Temple.

Middot 2:1 provides specific information regarding the relative areas of the courts that surrounded the Temple Court:

The Temple Mount measured five hundred cubits by five hundred cubits. Its largest [open] space was to the south, the next largest to the east, the third largest to the north, and its smallest [open space] was to the west; the place where its measure was greatest was where its use was greatest.

And, most conclusively of all, Josephus (*War* 5.184; *Ant.* 15.398) records that Herod's Temple was built on the top of the mountain. Using this information and placing the Temple Court on the 500-cubit-square platform, it soon becomes obvious that the Holy of Holies of the Temple has to be located over the Sakhra, the rock mass inside the Dome of the Rock, in order to conform to the requirements of the unequal sizes of the courts **(see Fig. 37)**. *Middot* 4:6 also tells us that the foundation of the Temple was 6 cubits (10 ft. or 3.05 m) high. If the Temple was placed anywhere else, higher foundations would have been needed to create a level platform for the Temple.

The size of the courts can be measured on the plan. Going counterclockwise, from south to west, they are 250, 213, 115 and 100 cubits, respectively—all of which surprisingly agree with those given by Tosefot Yom Tov in his commentary on *Middot* 2:1 dating from the sixteenth century.

Fig. 51

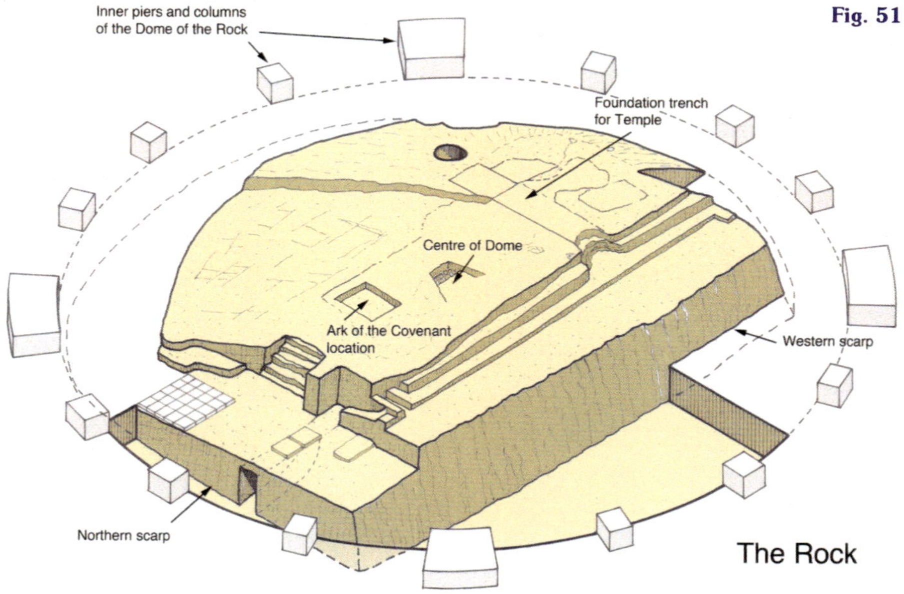

The Rock

The Rock

To refine this proposal, it was necessary to analyze the Sakhra, the Rock that is visible inside the Dome of the Rock. The Dome of the Rock consists of a circular dome-bearing drum, surrounded by two octagonal walls.

Both the central high drum rests on piers and pillars as does the inner ambulatory. The whole building is constructed round the Rock of biblical association **(Fig. 50)**. It takes an exercise of the imagination to realize that this Rock is actually the top of Mount Moriah, where Abraham was sent to sacrifice his son Isaac. We also saw earlier that, according to Jewish tradition, it was the same place where David later built an altar on the threshing floor of Araunah the Jebusite. As threshing floors are never built on the peak of a mountain but rather a little to the east, the Rock must have been the place where Solomon built the Holy of Holies, so that the altar would have stood between the Dome of the Chain and the eastern arcade.

On entering the Dome of the Rock, the western face of the Rock with its flat top is visible behind the wooden fence **(Fig. 51)**. On this side are two long steps carved apparently by the Crusaders as foundations for a broad stairway that led up to the top of the Rock on which they built a large marble altar. At the time of writing, there is a large black sign with the word "Allah" standing on a part of the Rock that is of great antiquity, constituting a vital element in the Temples of Jerusalem.

Fig. 50

The Rock inside the Dome of the Rock is the top of Mount Moriah

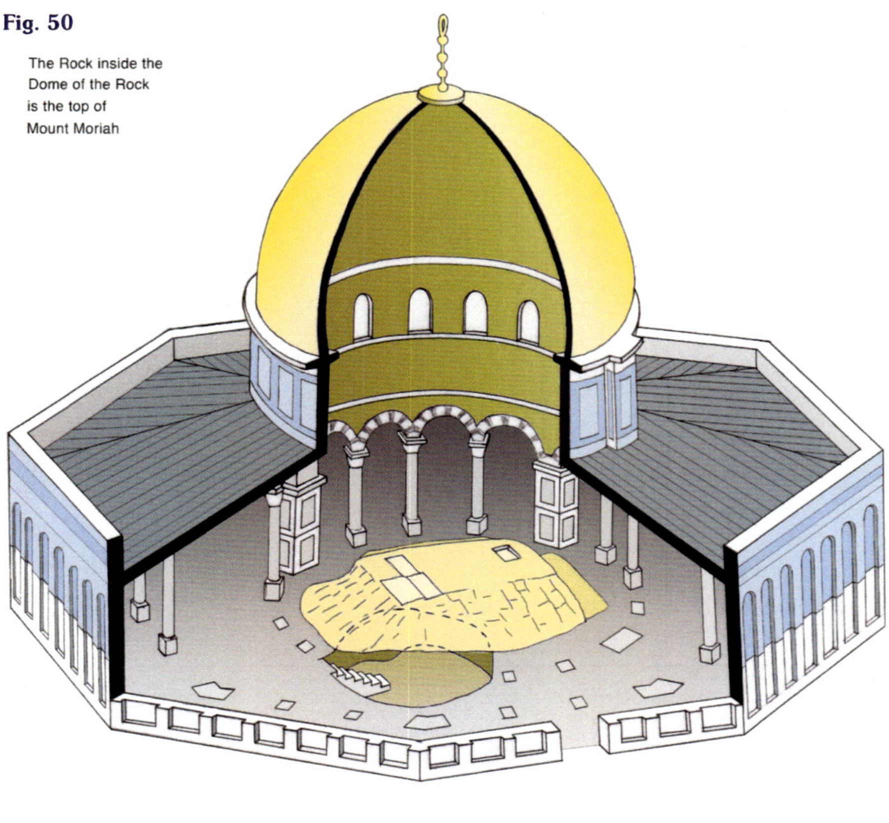

On the south of the Rock, is an opening to an underground cave known as *al-Maghara*. This was a small natural cave, enlarged by the Crusaders and used to commemorate the angel's announcement to Zacharias that he would have a son (Luke 1:13). A hole was cut in the rocky ceiling to let the smoke from candles and incense escape. Some have suggested that there might be another cave below the floor, the so-called *Bir al-Arwah* or the Well of Souls, but there is no evidence for this. On the contrary, an archaeologist who was present during renovation work a few decades ago noted that when the floor tiles had been pulled up, only rock was seen a few inches below, with no entrance to another cave.

Standing at the eastern side of the Rock and looking west, two flat rectangular areas cut in the rock can be observed. The author has identified these as foundation trenches for the south wall of the Holy of Holies of Solomon's Temple **(Fig. 52)**. They were cut to create a level surface on which to place the

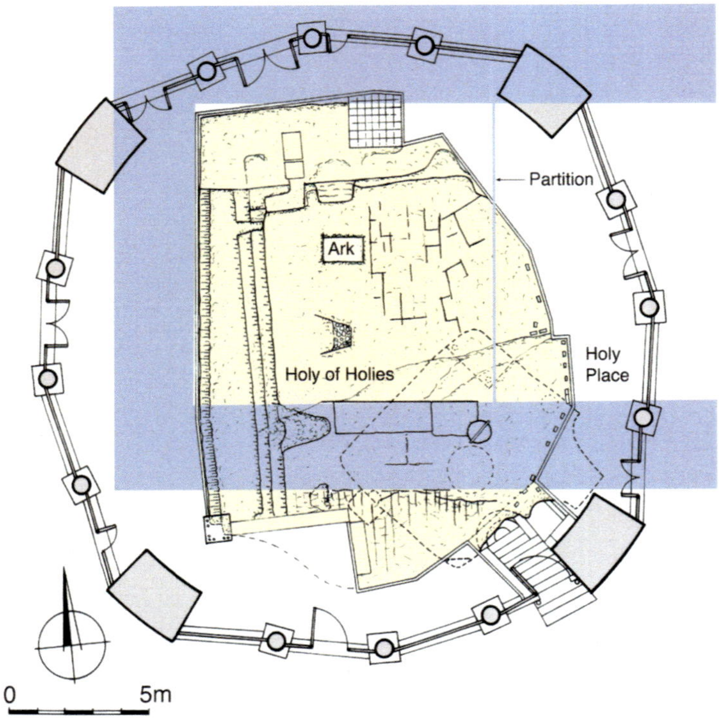

Fig. 52. *The location of Solomon's Temple relative to the Rock. The temple walls are indicated in blue.*

foundation stones of the Temple. On the eastern side, the Rock slopes down and quarry marks can be seen on its surface where the Crusaders had hewn off pieces to be sold as relics for their weight in gold. The upper level of the Rock can be better appreciated by examining the photograph (below) that was taken from high up under the dome **(Fig. 53)**. Two depressions are visible in the northern part. An artificially cut trapezoid indentation is located on a spot that can be calculated to be the very center of the Dome of the Rock. The most logical purpose for this was as the central pivot from which the plan of the Dome of the Rock was set out. Just to the north of this is a rectangular depression (where the black sign reading "Allah" has been placed).

This latter feature was the final one in a series of clues that allow us to decipher the history of the Rock on its lunar-like rocky surface. Using the flat areas on the south of the Rock together with the western and northern rock scarps, we can locate the original foundation walls of the Temple. The distance between the southern foundation trench and the northern rock scarp measured exactly 20 cubits (34 ft./10.5 m), the biblical dimensions given for the square Holy of Holies in 1 Kings 6:20. The measurements for the rectangular basin appeared at first to be equal to those of the Ark of the Covenant (Ex. 25:10), which were 1.5 ×2.5 cubits (2 ft. 7 in.×4 ft. 4 in. or 79×131 cm), with the longitudinal axis coinciding with that of the Temple. However, a photogrammetric analysis showed that, although the length of the depression was exactly the same as that of the Ark of the Covenant (4 ft. 4 in. or 1.31 m), the width was 1.00 m or 3 feet 3 inches, instead of the expected 80 cm or 2 feet 7 inches **(Fig. 54)**. This impression was apparently made wider than the size of the Ark of the Covenant to accommodate the placing of the Deuteronomy Scroll next to it, as the Levites had been commanded to do by Moses in Deuteronomy 31:26:

> *Take this book of the Law and put it in [by] the side of the Ark of the Covenant of the LORD your God that it may be there for a witness against thee.*

King Solomon records having "made a place" for the Ark in his Temple (1 Kings 8:20–21). It is logical that such a sacred object could not be left to wobble about on the rocky surface that the Scripture reveals to have been left unfloored (see earlier), but would need a stable base on which to stand. In addition to this, the indentation is located exactly in the center of the original projected Holy of Holies. These clues, together with others, provided the basis for an analysis of the Rock and confirmed the placing of the Temple on the summit of Mount Moriah, as recorded by Josephus.

On the Day of Atonement, the High Priest would have walked up the eastern ramp to reach the Holy of Holies that, in Solomon's time, was separated from the Holy Place by a set of olive wooden doors (1 Kings 6:31,32). The Deuteronomy Scroll written by Moses lay next to the Ark (Deut. 31:26). After a period of neglect, this scroll was found by Hilkiah the High Priest when he cleansed the Temple on orders of King Josiah (2 Kings 22:8).

Ezekiel's Temple and the Temple Scroll

We saw earlier that Hezekiah appears to have removed the

Fig. 53 *(left). The Rock as viewed from inside the Dome of the Rock.*

Fig. 54 *(below). A close-up view of the "Mark of the Ark" (photo Marcio Teixeira)*

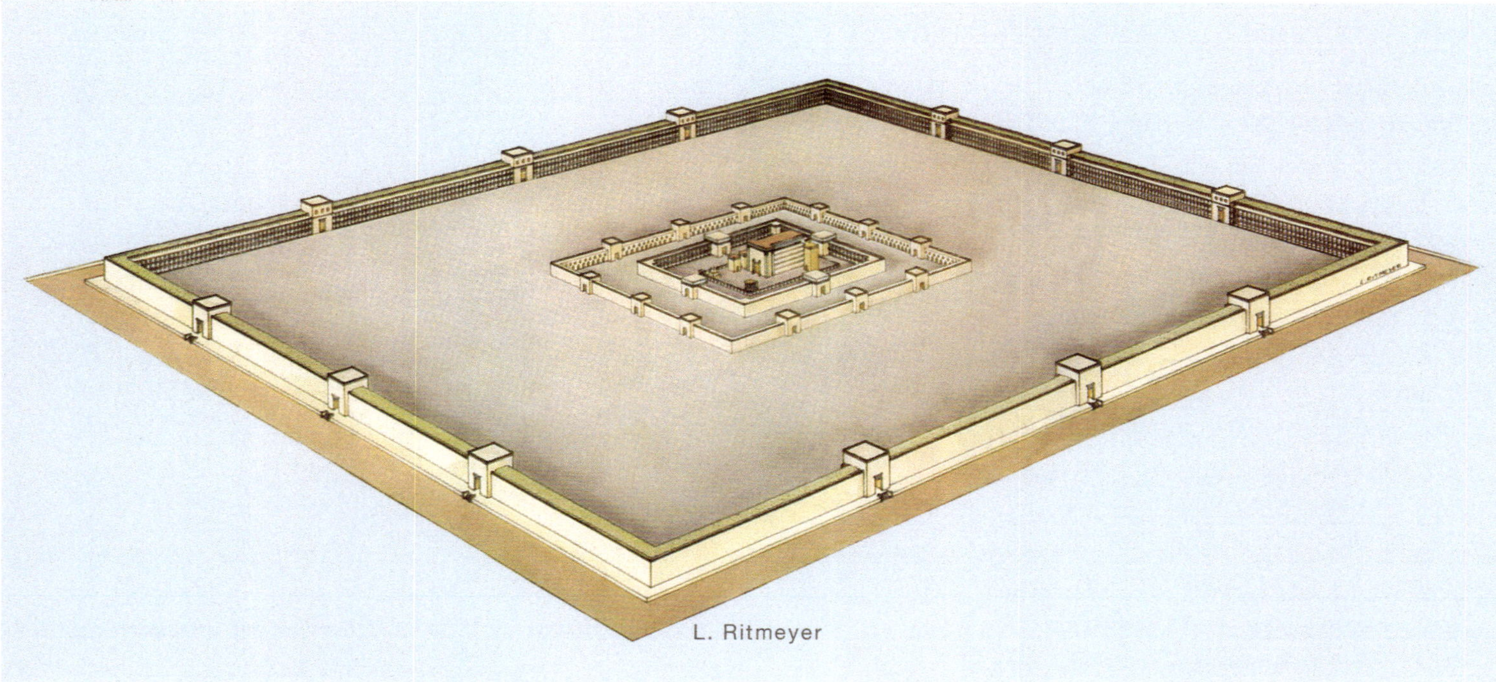

Fig. 55. *Reconstruction drawing of the square Temple court.*

Solomonic royal complex, thus separating it from the sacred area. This action may have been motivated by the description of God's anger in the prophecy of Ezekiel 43:8. Here the prophet describes the reason for God's displeasure as:

> *their setting of their threshold by my thresholds, and their post by my posts, and the wall between me and them, they have even defiled my holy name by their abominations that they have committed: wherefore I have consumed them in mine anger.*

The square Temple platform that resulted from the reforms of Hezekiah may have provided the model for another of the ancient records that describe a square Temple Court, measuring 500 cubits on each side, namely the Temple Scroll (*11Q19*)[31]. This scroll was acquired by the late Prof. Yigael Yadin in 1967[32] and describes three concentric courts **(Fig. 55).** The layout of the three concentric courts indicates different spheres of holiness. The Inner Court was described first, as it was holier than the other two courts. The Inner Court was for the priests (*11Q19 35.5–9*), the Middle Court for male Israelites (*11Q19 39.7–10*) and the Outer Court open to all Israelites, including women and children (*11Q19 40.5–6*). The measurements of the outer walls of the Middle Court were, according to Yadin, 480 cubits square, but he realized that this measurement was probably an internal measurement only[33]. Johann Maier[34] and others have suggested that the external measurements, including the outer walls, were 500 cubits each side. The size of this Middle Court would then be identical to that of *har habbayit*, the Temple Mount in Jerusalem of *Middot* 2:1.

In the Book of Ezekiel, chapters 40 and 41, another square Temple Mount is mentioned. According to this description, the inner Temple complex also measured 500 cubits each side. This is based on the fact that there were two sets of gates, each 50 cubits long, separated by a courtyard that measured 100 cubits. The inner set of gates was arranged around an inner court that was 100 cubits four-square. A square of 500 cubits was thus formed, with the Temple standing to the west of the inner court. It appears reasonable to suggest that the writer, the prophet Ezekiel, who was taken captive in Judea and exiled to Babylon, was familiar with these dimensions of the Temple Mount and therefore his Temple description supports a pre-exilic construction date for the square Temple platform. This 500-cubit-square inner complex of Ezekiel's Temple was surrounded by a vast square outer court that measured 500 reeds or 3,000 cubits (Ezekiel 42:16–20). This is almost double the size of the Outer Court of the Temple Scroll. Several scholars have tried to draw up the plan of this future temple[35].

For our purpose, however, we focus on the inner complex of 500 cubits, which is identical to the measurements of *Middot* and the Temple Scroll. If indeed the square Temple Mount dates from the time of Hezekiah, then the circumstances under which it was created may help us understand the significance of the measurement of the Middle Court of the Temple Scroll. As mentioned above, in order to build this square platform, Hezekiah had to dismantle the Solomonic palace complex with all its adjacent buildings. This royal and military complex was built right next to the Temple. As history has shown, the royal household (e.g., Queen Athaliah and Kings Uzziah and Ahaz) tried on several occasions to control the temple services and the priesthood. By dismantling this royal complex, Hezekiah effectively separated state from religion. This was also the purpose of the Temple Scroll. Lawrence Schiffman[36] described it as follows:

> *Extensive laws deal with the sacrificial procedure and with ritual purity and impurity. Here we see a general tendency to describe additional ways to protect the sanctuary from impurity.*

As the subject of the Temple Scroll and other Dead Sea Scrolls was the renewal of a purified priesthood and temple service, free from political interference, we ask if it is possible that the redactor of the Temple Scroll used Hezekiah's reforms and his Temple platform construction as an inspiration for his composition. And did its use of the 500-cubit square show that this form was looked upon as an ideal architectural and sacred entity?

THE POST-EXILIC TEMPLE

Following the Babylonian Exile, the altar was first rebuilt (Ezra 3:2,3), and then the foundation of the temple was laid (Ezra 3:10). There is no reason to doubt that these foundations followed the same orientation as the previous temple, as the foundation trenches were preserved in the Rock (as they are to this day). Due to the opposition of the local population, it took twenty years to complete the building. It did not match the splendor of its predecessor, as witnessed by the reaction of the older people who still remembered the First Temple:

But many of the priests and Levites and chief of the fathers, who were ancient men, that had seen the first house, when the foundation of this house was laid before their eyes, wept with a loud voice; and many shouted aloud for joy: So that the people could not discern the noise of the shout of joy from the noise of the weeping

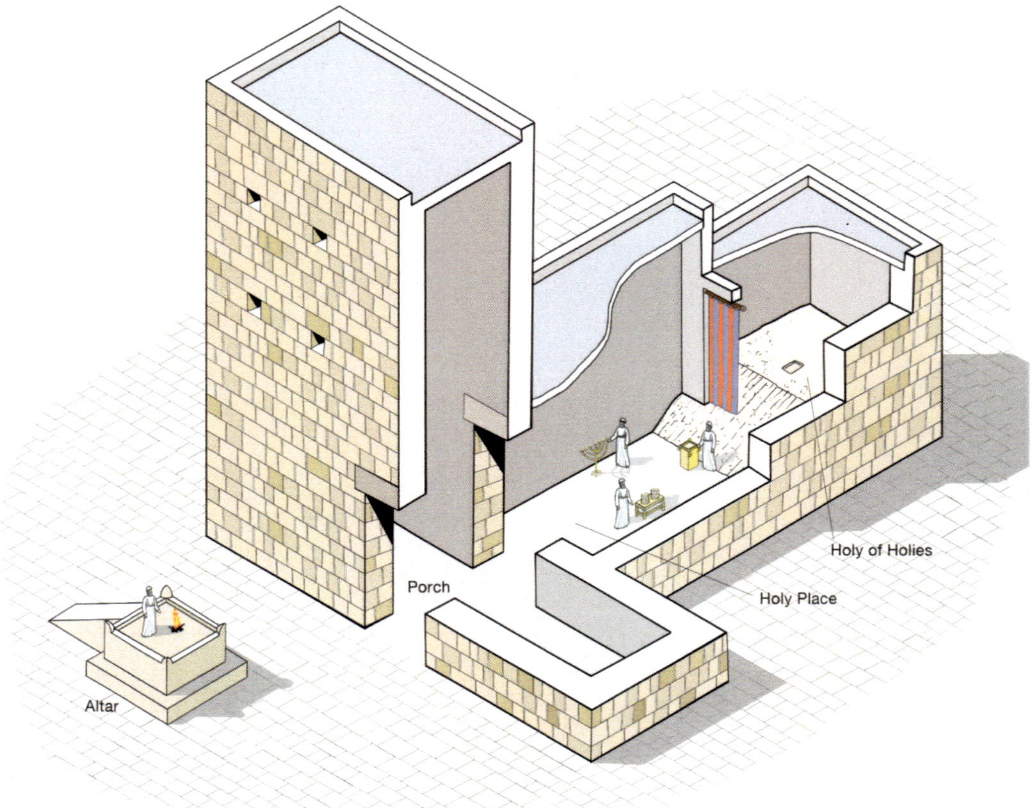

Fig. 56. *Cutaway reconstruction of the Temple built by Zerubbabel and Jeshua.*

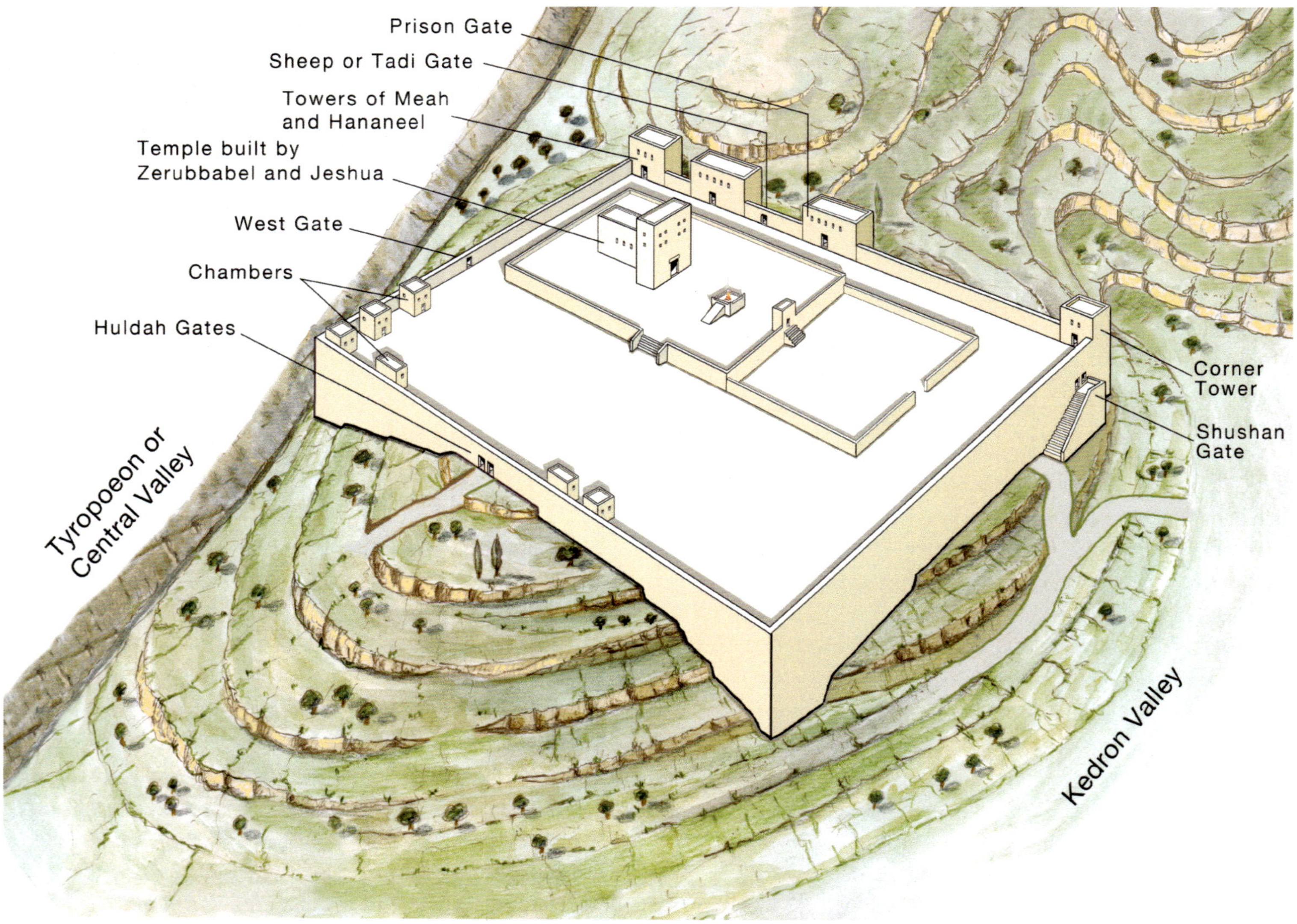

Fig. 57. *The Temple Mount in the Post-Exilic period.*

of the people: for the people shouted with a loud shout, and the noise was heard afar off. (Ezra 3:12–13)

After a period of some twenty years, the Temple building was completed (Ezra 6:15) **(Fig. 56)**. The only information given about the Second Temple is that it was 60 cubits high and wide. These measurements presumably referred to its façade, as no measurements for length are provided.

The Post-Exilic Temple Mount

The reconstruction of the Temple Mount itself was carried out under the supervision of Nehemiah and is partially described in Nehemiah 3 **(Fig. 57)**. Our location of the square Temple Mount has led to the possible discovery of the remains of a tower at its northeast corner. Certain other towers and a gate are known to have existed along the northern wall of the Temple Mount during the First Temple period. Identifying the location of these structures would also further strengthen our suggestion that the construction of the square Temple Mount took place during the First Temple period.

The Northeast Tower

The possible discovery of the remains of a tower at the northeast corner of the square Temple Mount has been described above. The Book of Nehemiah (chap. 3) describes the building and the restoration of the city walls of Jerusalem. At the end of chapter 3, while describing the northern part of the eastern city wall, Nehemiah mentions that certain merchants repaired a stretch of wall, *"over against the gate Miphkad and the going up* (aliyah) *of the corner"* (Neh. 3:31–32). As a rule, *aliyah* is translated as "chamber" in the Old Testament, and in one case (2 Sam. 18:33), *aliyah* refers to the upper chamber of a gate. It could, therefore, also refer to an upper chamber or turret of a tower, located at a corner between the gate *Miphkad* and the Sheep Gate, the last structure mentioned in this chapter.

The sources do not give the location of the gate *Miphkad*. In the prophecy of Ezekiel's Temple *"the appointed place of the house"* (*miphqad habbayit*), where the sin offering is burnt, is located outside the Temple. This may be an indication that the gate *Miphkad* of Nehemiah's time could have been located outside the Temple, and may therefore have been a gate in the eastern city wall, near the approach to the eastern gate of the Temple Mount.

The text does not indicate whether the corner referred to was the northeast angle of the square Temple Mount or a corner of the city wall. The archaeological remains in the area of the Golden Gate indicate that the city wall found by Warren **(Fig. 58)** was curved and had no corner built into it, and that the only tower found in this area was part of the square platform. Our suggested reconstruction of this area **(Fig. 59)** shows that the city wall linked up with the Eastern Wall near the northeast corner of the square Temple Mount and that the tower belongs to the square platform. Although this tower is architecturally an integral part of the Temple Mount, its location near the termination of the Eastern Wall closely associates it with this city wall. Additionally, the northern wall of the square Temple Mount would have effectively doubled as a city wall, as there was no independent city wall skirting the north of the Temple Mount. This then is most probably the reason why the

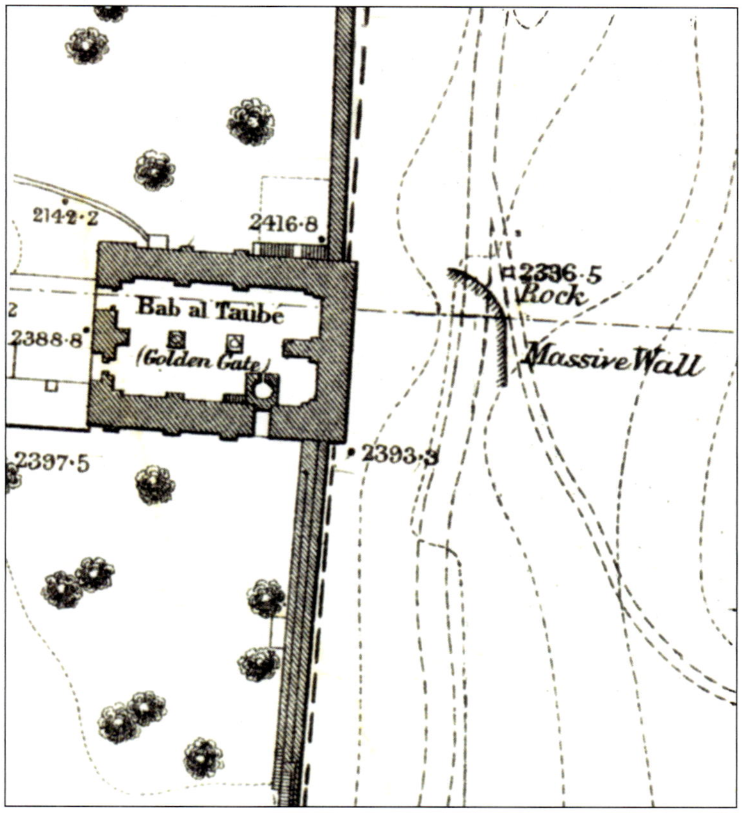

Fig. 58 *(above). Warren's plan of the city wall.*

Fig. 59 *(below). Reconstruction model of the area.*

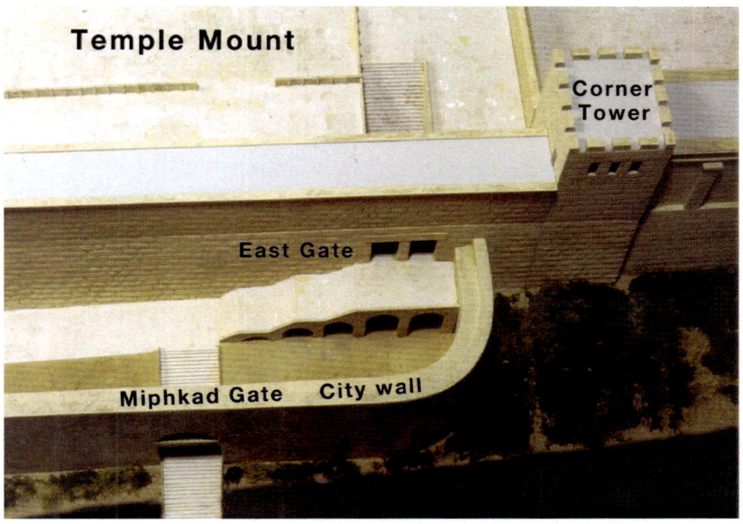

northeast tower is mentioned in the description of the city walls. We propose therefore that the remains of this tower be identified with the upper chamber of the corner, which was located near the gate *Miphkad*, according to Nehemiah's record.

The Towers of Hananeel and Meah

The existence of defensive towers in the northern wall of the square Temple Mount during the siege of Pompey in 63 B.C. was recorded by Josephus (*Ant.* 14.61). According to his narrative, some towers must have stood close to the southern side of the excavated ditch. Because of the limited space between the northern wall of the square Temple Mount and the excavated ditch, it seems reasonable to assume that these towers were attached to the square Temple Mount. If this was the case, they could be identified with the Hasmonean *Baris*, which according to Josephus stood at the northwest angle of the Temple (*Ant.* 15.403).

Fig. 60. *Reconstruction model of the Temple Mount in the time of Nehemiah.*

It is interesting to note that the Tower of Hananeel, according to Nehemiah's description of the city wall[37], also stood at or near the northwest corner of the Temple Mount. This tower already existed at the end of the First Temple period, according to the biblical record of Jeremiah 31:38 and Zechariah 14:10. Hananeel's Tower must have been destroyed during the Babylonian conquest of 586 B.C., and later rebuilt by Nehemiah **(Fig. 60)**. The *Baris* was apparently the successor of the Tower of Hananeel, as it occupied the same location at the northwest corner of the square Temple Mount. This would indicate that at least the northwest corner of Nehemiah's Temple Mount coincided with that of the pre-exilic period.

Continuing this line of thought, we suggest that this fortress at the northwest corner may have had twin towers, the eastern one of which may have been the Tower Meah, or the "Tower of the Hundred" (Neh. 3:1; 12:39), as this tower is always mentioned together with the Tower of Hananeel. It is possible, as already suggested by Simons[38], that these two towers are respectively the eastern and the western tower of a fortress located at the northwest corner of the pre-exilic Temple Mount.

The Ptolemaic Akra

The *Baris* was constructed at the northwest corner of the square Temple Mount by Hyrcanus in c. 134 B.C. However, in *Antiquities* 12.133, 138, Josephus mentions another fortress or citadel that was built prior to this. He refers to a citadel, or *Akra*, from which a Ptolemaic garrison was ejected by the forces of Antiochus III in 198 B.C. This citadel was probably built soon after the invasion of the region in the beginning of the third century B.C. A citadel near the Temple Mount would have consolidated the Ptolemaic hold over Jerusalem against the threat of the Seleucids. In this context, one would expect this citadel to be located on the north of the Temple Mount, where it could best serve against Syrian attacks from this direction.

We suggest that the remains of the ancient towers of Hananeel and Meah probably still existed at the beginning of the Ptolemaic domination of the Holy Land, although by then their names may have been forgotten. These towers, situated at the strategic northwest corner of the Temple Mount, may have been rebuilt as the Ptolemaic *Akra*.

The Sheep Gate and the Prison Gate

Archaeological evidence for another tower in the northern wall of the square Temple Mount may be found in the so-called Tank 29, investigated by Warren. It consists of a 70-foot-long passage going east to west with four bays on the south that have medieval pointed vaults resting on piers attached to the northern wall of the platform. The southern parts of these piers are cut out of the rock and project from the northern end of the raised platform. Warren wrote about these southern bays[39]: "*The bays are from 11 feet to 13 feet span, and about 16 feet deep. The piers are 3.5 feet thick.*" We are especially interested in his descriptive account of this area, where he writes[40]:

> *The southern side of these bays is scarped rock, and on it the wall supporting the northern edge of the Mosque platform is built. Portions of the piers are also scarped from the rock, which appears to shelve down rapidly to the north; so that, if the earth and these vaults were removed, the northern end of the Mosque platform would present the appearance of a perpendicularly scarped rock with excrescences on its face 3 feet 6 inches thick, 12 feet apart, and projecting about 6 feet.*

Warren was able to investigate only the visible area, but noted that both ends were blocked by fill. There may therefore be more cells cut out of the bedrock than the four he saw. These bedrock projections are apparently part of the substructure of a building that once stood above them and could be accessed from the Temple Mount.

In the record of Nehemiah 12:39, the Sheep Gate and the Prison (*Matarah*) Gate are mentioned after the towers of Hananeel and Meah. Could these bedrock cells discovered in Cistern 29 have been used as a prison? If this feature indeed points to the former location of the Prison Gate, and we follow the circuit described in

Fig. 61. *The Tadi Gate.*

Nehemiah 12, where the Sheep Gate is mentioned just before the Prison Gate, then the latter and the twin towers of Hananeel and Meah would have flanked this same Sheep Gate.

The Tadi Gate

According to *Middot* 1:3, there was a gate in the north wall of the 500-cubit-square Temple Mount called the *Tadi* Gate, which apparently was never used. *Middot* 1:9 indicates that this gate had a subterranean passage, and 2:3 states further that the gate had a lintel composed of two stones that leaned against each other **(Fig. 61)**. An interesting example of such a construction was found in the passageway at the top of the stepped tunnel that leads down to Warren's Shaft in the City of David[41]. The roof of the entry tunnel is made of stone slabs whose tops lean against each other, forming a continuous gable **(Fig. 62)**. We propose that the lintel construction of the Tadi Gate was probably also gabled in similar fashion. Warren already suggested that this Tadi Gate of *Middot* may have been located in the northern wall of the raised platform[42] and was connected with Cistern 1. This cistern is a tunnel-like passageway, 130 feet (39.5 m) long, 24 feet (7.30 m) wide, with its floor located 30 feet (9.10 m) below the surface of the platform. The side walls are cut out of the bedrock and the roof is a stone vault. The northern end is closed with a rough stone wall and the passageway may also have extended further to the south. It appears therefore that this structure, originally built as an underground passageway, as its shape suggests, was plastered over and turned into a cistern much later, probably during the early Muslim or Crusader period. When Herod the Great extended the platform to the north, any gate at the end of this passageway would have been buried underground, thus rendering it useless, as *Middot* 1:3 indeed indicates.

Another cistern complex nearby, Cistern 3, also has a passageway on its east side, concerning which Warren[43] wrote:

> *The production of the main gallery of No. 3 cuts the production of the gallery of No. 1, if both are produced northward, just at the north wall of the platform, where the subterranean gate Tadi appears most probably to have been placed, as shown on the plan (Pl. 6). The ground in this vicinity has a hollow sound.*

The northern parts of both these passages are blocked by similar-looking walls that made it impossible for Warren to investigate their relation to the northern wall of the Muslim platform. Warren had suggested that this cistern may have been the bathhouse of the Temple. Schick[44], who also investigated this cistern, discounted this possibility, as he found no remains of steps leading to the surface. In a forthcoming companion volume to this publication, we shall see that this cistern is indeed located below the Chamber of the Hearth, from which priests could descend into the bathhouse. The entrance would have been located a short distance to the north of the blocked passageway.

The location of Cistern 1 is of interest because it forms part of a clear north-south axis through the Sakhra and the underground passageways of the Double Gate. From an architectural point of view, this shows that both passageways were designed at the same time, and that both are related to the Rock.

It is tempting to speculate that the Mishnaic Tadi Gate stood in the same place as the pre-exilic Sheep Gate. The meaning of *Tadi* remains unknown. It has been suggested[45] that *Tadi* is a misreading of *Tali* or *Taleh*, which means *Lamb* in Hebrew. In that case, it would not be difficult to see the connection between the Sheep and the "Lamb" Gate.

Fig. 62. *The roof of the entry tunnel leading to Warren's Shaft.*

THE HELLENISTIC TEMPLE MOUNT

In *Antiquities* 11.325–339, Josephus records a visit to the Temple by Alexander the Great after his capture of Gaza in 332 B.C. Here, the Jewish historian has him sacrificing in the Temple under the guidance of the High Priest. Although this may be mere legend, the story points to the perpetuation of the Temple services following their revival after the return from exile in Babylon. After the death of Alexander, Judea was governed by the Ptolemies of Egypt, who were tolerant of Jewish religious practice.

Simon the High Priest

In 200 B.C., some restoration work on the Temple Mount was carried out by the High Priest Simon, son of Onias, according to the apocryphal work of Ben Sira, called *Ecclesiasticus*. The work is described as follows:

> *It was the High Priest Simon son of Onias who repaired the Temple during his lifetime and in his day fortified the sanctuary. He laid the foundations of the double height, the high buttresses of the Temple precincts. In his day the water cistern was excavated, a reservoir as huge as the sea.*[46]

It is clear from this text that the bulk of these works were concerned with the repair and strengthening of existing structures, although no archaeological remains can be demonstrated as belonging to this enterprise[47]. The need for such repair work is not surprising as, after three centuries of service, the Temple and its precincts would have been in need of repair.

I have reasoned elsewhere[48] that the original function of the water cisterns on the Temple Mount was to supply building stones. This is evident from the rough staircases that were found in the large cisterns. These stairs were used for hauling up the stones, while later on, after the walls and floor were plastered, water was drawn up through manholes that were made in the ceiling of these quarries. Only a few of the cisterns can be classified as being as "large as the sea." There are two cisterns that are called by that name, Cistern 8—"the great sea" and Cistern 7—"the sea." The entrance to Cistern 8 is located south of the square Temple Mount and inside the area of the Hasmonean extension. It is reasonable to suggest therefore that this cistern provided the building blocks for the Hasmonean extension. Cistern 7 is located closer to the Temple complex and we suggest therefore that this cistern was the "reservoir as huge as the sea" from which the building material was extracted for the building activities of Simon.

The Seleucid Akra

Control of the city was won from the Ptolemies by the Greek Seleucids from Syria in around 200 B.C. The Seleucid dynasty was determined to force the Jews to accept Hellenism. It was the sacrifice of a pig on the Temple altar by the Seleucid ruler Antiochus IV Epiphanes that sparked off the revolt by the Maccabee brothers. Their bloodline evolved into the Hasmonean dynasty that established an independent Jewish state lasting from 164 to 63 B.C.

Simon the Maccabee demolished the hated Akra, a fortress that the Seleucids had built to the south of the Temple Mount so that a Macedonian garrison could control the Jewish population **(Fig. 63)**.

Following the capture of the Akra in 141 B.C., Simon razed the fortress to the ground and then, according to 1 Maccabees 13:52,

> *He strengthened the fortifications of the Temple Mount by the side of the Akra, and took up residence there with his men....*

and 1 Maccabees 14:37,

> *He settled Jewish soldiers in it and fortified it as a protection for the country and city, and heightened the walls of Jerusalem.*

This would seem to indicate that a large area, previously occupied

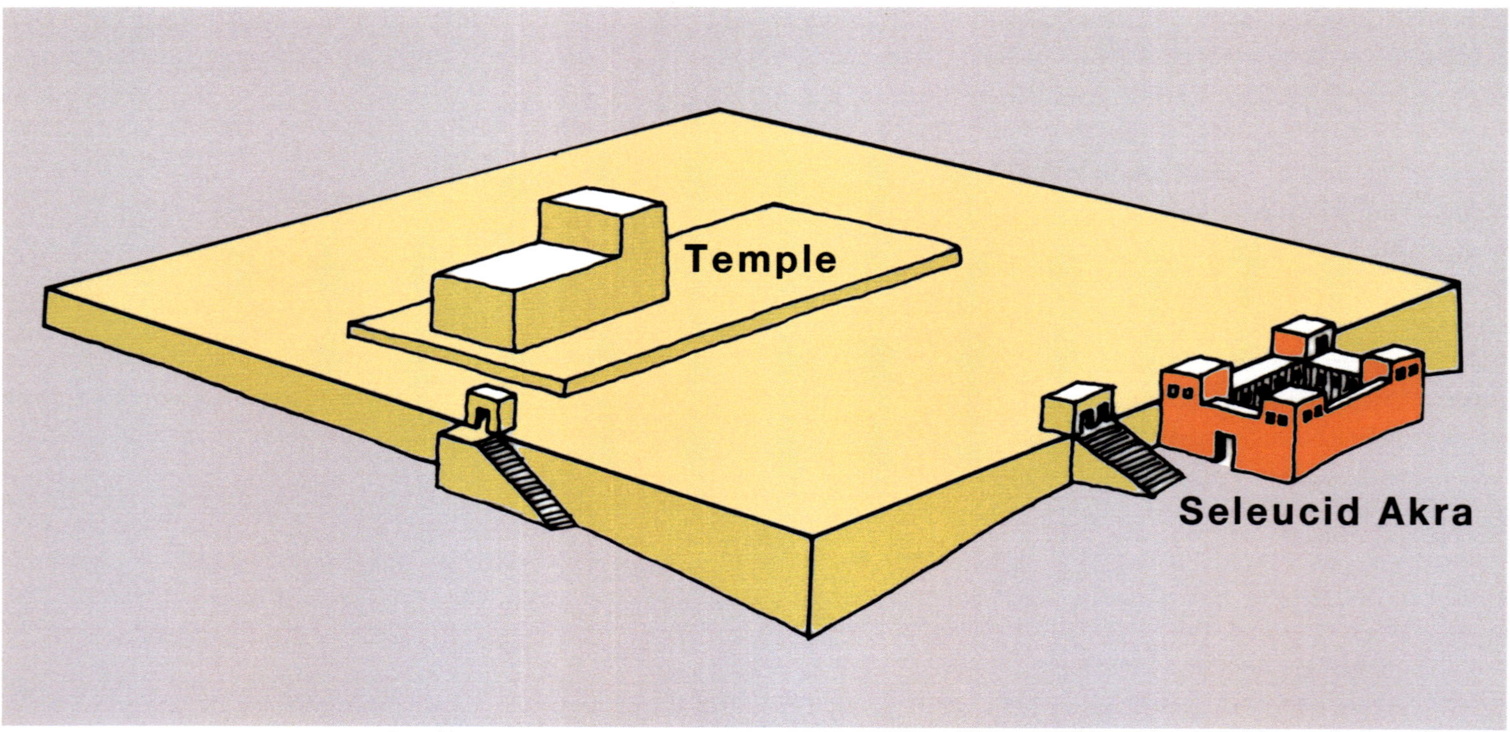

Fig. 63. *Reconstruction drawing of the Seleucid Akra south of the Temple Mount.*

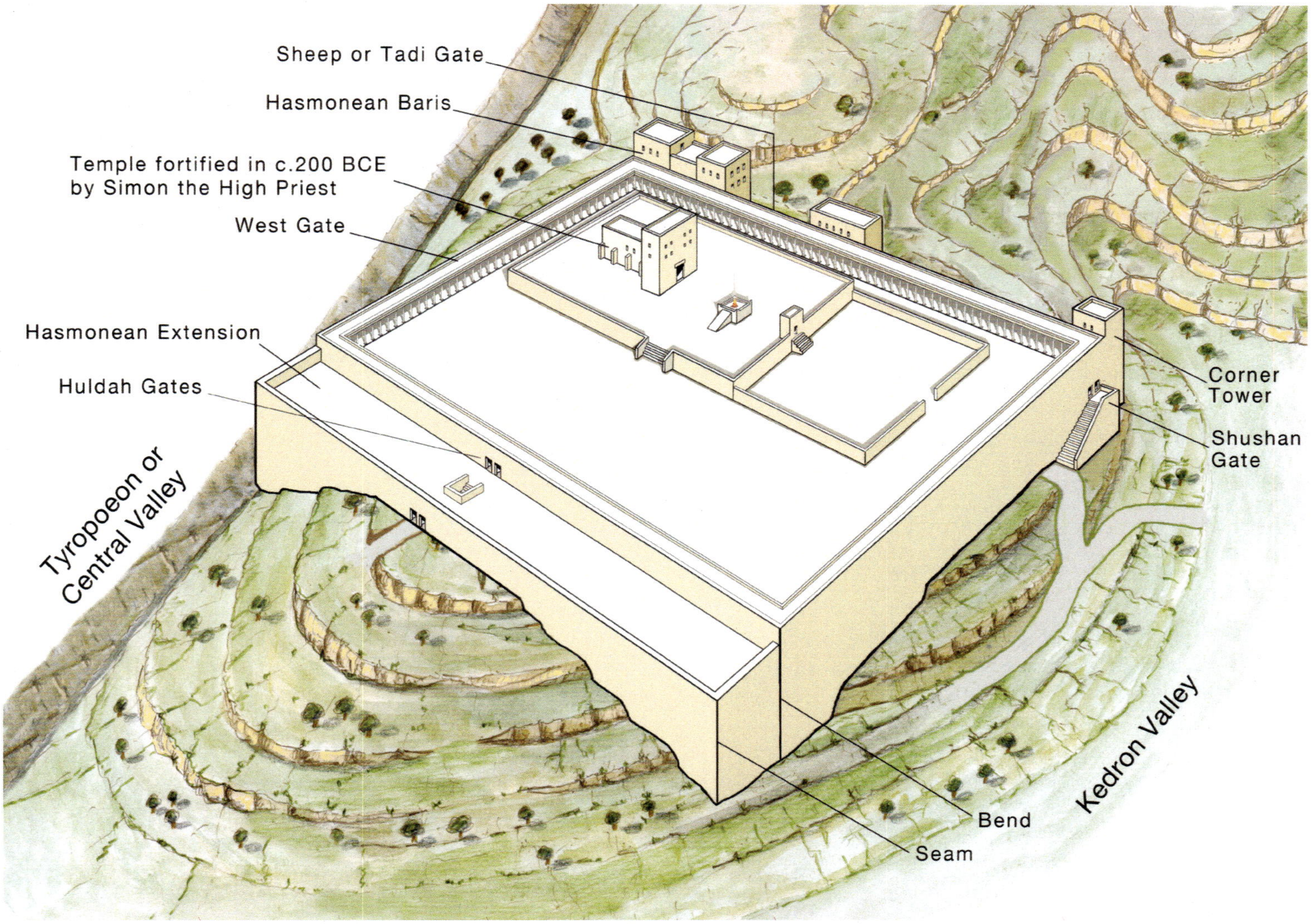

Fig. 64. *The Temple Mount in the Hellenistic-Hasmonean period.*

by the Akra, was built south of the Temple Mount and incorporated into it. After this extension to the south, the Temple was no longer square in shape **(Fig. 64)**.

Following the Maccabean rebellion, a fortress was constructed at the northwest corner of the square Temple Mount, to defend the mount against attacks from the north. It was called the Baris.

The Feast of Hanukkah

The consecration of the Temple by Judah the Maccabee, after Antiochus IV Epiphanes desecrated it in 167 B.C., is still celebrated today by the Jewish feast of Hanukkah. This commemorates the miracle of the Temple lights, when the cruse of oil containing only sufficient oil for one day, lasted for eight days. It is recorded in the New Testament that Jesus was almost stoned one wintry day during the feast of Hanukkah (John 10:22–39, where it is called the Feast of Dedication). This happened when Jesus was speaking with his disciples at Solomon's Porch which was the eastern portico of Herod's Temple Mount, while around them in the Temple precincts, the people celebrated God's intervention in the restoration of their place of worship. Today, commencing on the 25th of *Kislev*, the Jewish people light an eight-branched lampstand, called a *Hanukkiah* **(Fig. 65)**, on each of the eight nights of Hanukkah. Each branch represents one of the nights that the oil miraculously burned in the Temple. The lamp on the central ninth branch, which is called the *shamash*, is used to light the others.

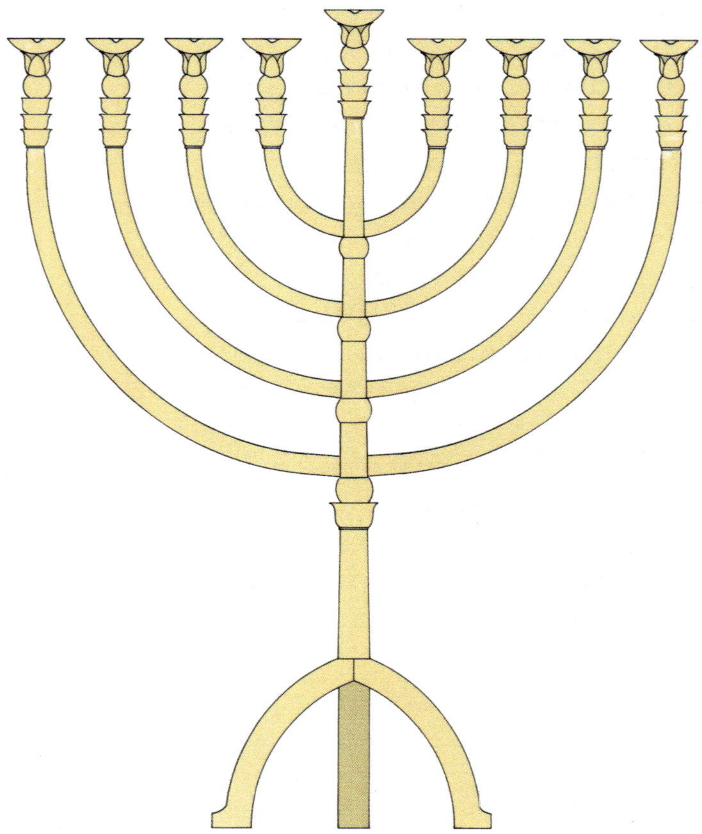

Fig. 65. *Eight-branched* Hanukkiah.

THE HASMONEAN TEMPLE MOUNT

As we have already suggested above, the masonry to the north of the vertical joint (popularly known as the *seam*), which is visible above ground, 105 feet 6 inches (32 m) from the southeast corner, appears to have been part of an enterprise to enlarge the square Temple Mount to the south **(Fig. 66)**. There is no doubt that this masonry is earlier than the Herodian masonry south of the *seam*. Although these stones are slightly smaller and shorter than the Herodian ones, they have been cut very precisely. Their margins are narrow and straight, tooled with a broad chisel, unlike the tooth-comb pick used by the Herodian masons. The bosses are flat and project much more than the Herodian ones. A careful examination of the stones to the immediate north of the *seam* shows that parts of their southernmost margins have been cut away in several places in order to create a better key for the Herodian stones that adjoin them to the south of the *seam* **(see Fig. 67)**. The stones to the immediate north of the *seam* were built as headers and stretchers, which is always indicative of a corner construction. We have suggested[49] that, historically, this type of masonry could best be ascribed to the building activities that took place during the time of Simon, the third son of Mattathias. Avigad[50] pointed out that the fortification of the Upper City carried out during the Hasmonean period was probably initiated by Jonathan the second son of Mattathias (160–142 B.C.) and completed by his brother Simon (142–134 B.C.).

There are indications that the remains of a corresponding Hasmonean Western Wall may still exist. Barclay's Gate is one of the four gates in the Herodian Western Wall described by Josephus (*Ant.* 15.396). A massive lintel stone in the Western Wall of the Herodian Temple Mount on the south side of the Western Wall Plaza testifies to the existence of an underground passageway. Unlike the underground tunnels in the Southern Wall, which are straight, the interior passage of Barclay's Gate is L-shaped. Wilson, who also inspected this underground space, suggested that this change in direction may have been caused because of the existence of "the original retaining wall of Solomon's Temple, which it was not thought necessary to remove when the area was enlarged by Herod."[51] He was not far from the truth. An examination of the L-shaped underground passage of Barclay's Gate shows that the first part begins at the gate and passes through the al-Burak Mosque in an easterly direction until it reaches a distance of 84 feet from the Western Wall inside Cistern 19. The passageway then turns south under a flat dome, and its continuation is found in the western part of Cistern 20 **(Fig. 68)**. A reconstruction drawing of the Herodian

Figs. 66 and 67. *Photograph and plan of the "seam" at the southern end of the Eastern Wall of the Temple Mount.*

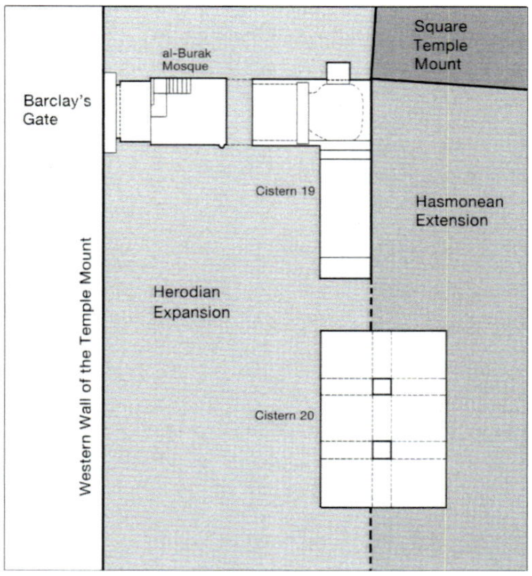

Fig. 68. *Plan of Cistern 20.*

Fig. 69

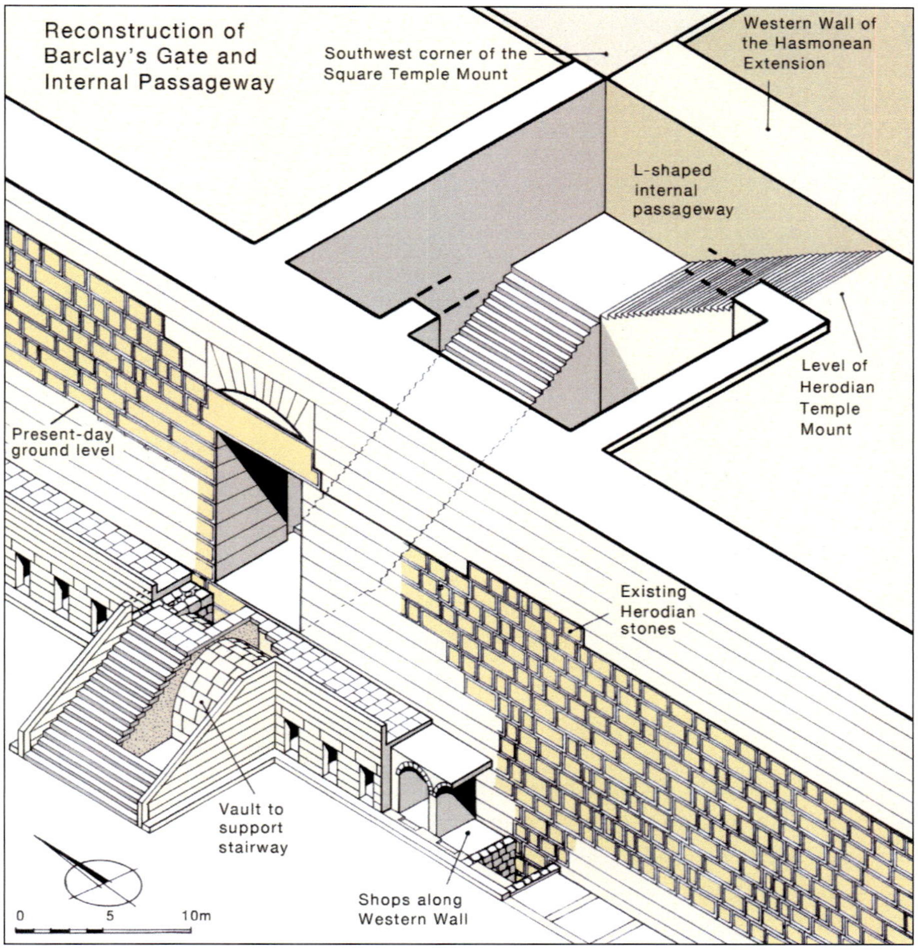

passageway inside Barclay's Gate shows that an L-shaped internal stairway eventually led up from a street along the Western Wall to the internal level of the Temple Mount **(Fig. 69)**.

The eastern wall of Cistern 19 and the wall supporting the two columns in Cistern 20 apparently form part of the Western Wall of the Hasmonean Temple Mount, which was built when the square platform was extended to the south following the destruction of the Akra. Cistern 20 is only 10 meters deep, which is less than the other large cisterns. It appears that when this cistern was dug, presumably in the Crusader period, judging by the vaulted roof construction, excavation work was halted when the preserved top of the Hasmonean wall was reached. At the southern end of this cistern, the bedrock is located some 70 feet (21 m) below **(Fig. 70)**. This points to the possibility that the southwest corner of the Hasmonean Temple Mount has been preserved to the considerable height of 70 feet (21 m). Assuming an average height of 1 meter for each stone course, there may still be twenty-one Hasmonean stone courses preserved along its southern wall. This would correspond closely to the twenty-two stone courses that have been preserved at the southeast corner of the Hasmonean extension[52]. The western Hasmonean wall would have been built against the southwest corner of the square Temple Mount. As the bedrock slopes up to the north, it can be inferred that the southwest corner of the square Temple Mount would have survived to a minimum height of 50 feet (15 m) or fifteen stone courses, which is only two courses less than the seventeen courses that have been preserved at the corresponding southeast corner.

The reason then for the L-shape of the underground stairway of Barclay's Gate was that Herod's builders conveniently built the southern part of this stairway alongside the still-existing remains of the Western Wall of the Hasmonean extension instead of piercing through it, which would have been a difficult and senseless operation.

It was this Hasmonean Temple Mount that existed at the time when Herod the Great became king. By extending this platform to the north, west and south, he doubled the size of the original square Temple Mount that was built by King Hezekiah. Although the works of Herod on the Temple Mount made it more difficult to investigate the earlier constructions, with the help of the historical sources and observations of the scant remains, it has been possible to have a better idea how the Temple Mount developed during the time of the Old Testament.

Fig. 70

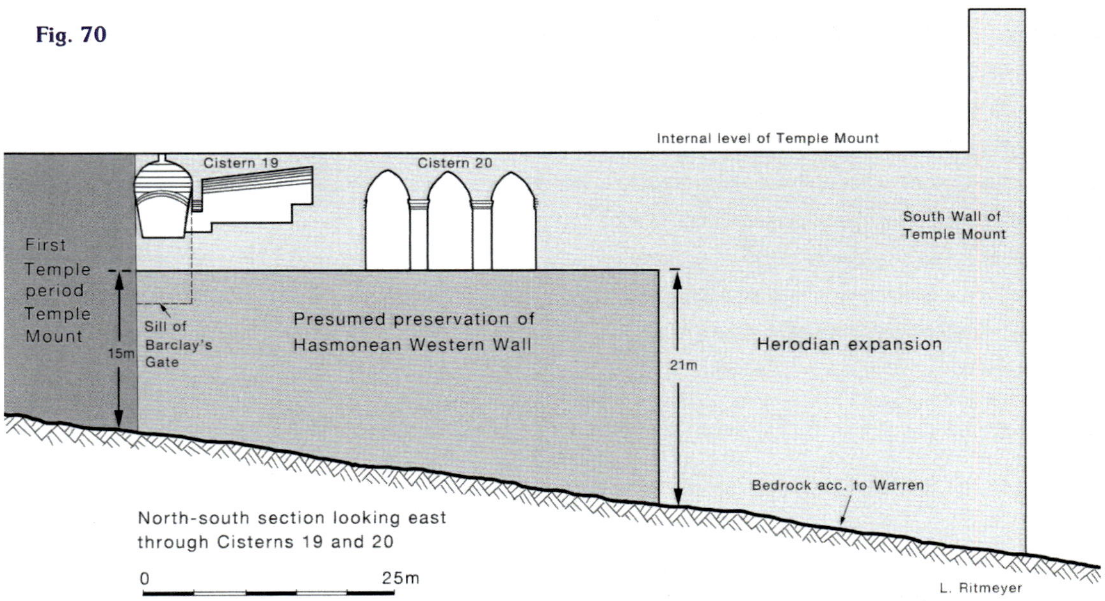

NOTES AND REFERENCES

1 Hamblin (2007) 13–14.

2 Parry, "The Garden of Eden: Prototype Sanctuary," in: Parry (1994), 126–151; Beale (2011), 617–621; Price (2012), 7–9.

3 See description of the Tabernacle in: Haran (1985), 149–165.

4 Vaux (1961), 297–300; Haran (1985), 246–259.

5 Cp. Ritmeyer (2000).

6 A collection of reconstruction drawings of Solomon's Temple appears in: Rosenau (1979).

7 Cp. Ritmeyer (2006), 279–294.

8 Alternatively, the Septuagint gives 25 cubits for the height of the *heikhal*, as does the Lucianic recension. If these texts could be relied upon, then the roofs of the *heikhal* and the *debir* would be on the same level. See de Vaux (1961), 314.

9 Fritz (1987), 45.

10 Reich, "Palaces and Residencies in the Iron Age: The Integration of Wooden Beams in Stone Construction," in: Kempinski and Reich, eds. (1992), 213.

11 Biran (1982), 20, Pl. 5.1.

12 Shea, W. H. (1999). "Jerusalem under Siege: Did Sennacherib Attack Twice?" in: *BAR* 25.6: 36–44, 64.

13 Mazar (1992), 106, 108.

14 See Geva (2014), "Jerusalem's Population in Antiquity: A Minimalist View," in: *Tel Aviv* 41 (2): 131–160.

15 In the historical context, the *birah* indicates the citadel of Jerusalem, i.e., the fortified Temple Mount. This term should not be confused with the later Baris of the Hasmonean period.

16 Ritmeyer (1992), 24–45, 64–65; Ritmeyer (2006), 139–206.

17 Ritmeyer (2006), 167.

18 Bahat argues that this gate was built in the Byzantine period, but the absence of any crosses in both its interior and exterior decoration makes this highly unlikely. See Bahat (2011), 87

19 Vogüé (1864), 12, Fig. 10.

20 Ritmeyer (2006), 177.

21 See: Ritmeyer (2006) 109, illustration at bottom of page.

22 These were first pointed out to me by Susan Rogers of the now defunct Temple Research Group.

23 Warren (1884), Pl. 12.

24 Ritmeyer (2006), 178–179.

25 Dunand (1969), 64–70.

26 Warren (1884), Plate 5.

27 Warren and Conder (1884), 229.

28 Kenyon (1974), 115.

29 Mazar (2011), 119.

30 Avigad (1983), 46–49; Geva (ed.), (2000), 37–130.

31 Yadin (Hebrew 1977, English 1983).

32 The acquisition of the scroll is told in: Yadin (1985), 8–55.

33 Yadin (1985), 148.

34 Maier (1989), 23–62.

35 Sulley (1921); Stevenson (1996); Schmitt and Laney (1997); Clorfene, (2005).

36 Schiffman (1994), 261.

37 Neh 3:1, 12:39. See also Smith (1907–08), vol. I, 201; vol. II, 261, 348, 460.

38 Simons (1952), 429, n.2.

39 Warren and Conder (1884), 224.

40 Wilson and Warren (1871), 219.

41 Shiloh (1984), 21, Pl. 39.1.

42 Warren and Conder (1884), 218.

43 Warren and Conder (1884), 218.

44 Schick (1887) 84–85.

45 Kaufman (1984–85), 97–108.

46 Ecclesiasticus 50.1–3.

47 Patrich mistakenly classified a post–Herodian stairway, located south of the raised platform of the Dome of the Rock (see Warren, Plate 5), as a "graded wall" (an unknown architectural term) and erroneously identified this archaeological remnant with the southern wall of Simon's building activities of about 200 B.C. See Patrich (2011), 571.

48 Ritmeyer (2006), 225–227.

49 Ritmeyer (2006), 211.

50 Avigad (1983), 72.

51 Wilson (1880), 20.

52 See: Ritmeyer (2006), 104.

BIBLIOGRAPHY

Avigad, N. (1980 [Hebrew]; 1983 [English]). *Discovering Jerusalem* (Jerusalem, Nashville).

Bahat, D. (2011). *The Carta Jerusalem Atlas* (Jerusalem).

Beale, G. K. (2011). *A New Testament Biblical Theology: The Unfolding of the Old Testament in the New* (Grand Rapids).

Biran, A. (1982). "Ha-Mitham ha-Pulhani be-Dan" in: *Eretz-Yisrael* 16, 15–43 [Hebrew].

Chaim Clorfene, C. (2005). *The Messianic Temple* (Jerusalem).

Danby, H. (1933).*The Mishnah, translated from the Hebrew with Introduction and Explanatory notes* (Oxford).

Dunand, M. (1969). "Byblos, Sidon, Jérusalem. Monuments apparentés des temps Achéménides" in: *Congress Volume* (Rome, 1968), *Vetus Testamentum Supplement* 17, 64–70 (Leiden).

Fritz, V. (1987). "What Can Archaeology Tell Us about Solomon's Temple" in: *BAR* 13.4, 38–49.

Geva, H., ed. (2000). *Jewish Quarter Excavations in the Old City of Jerusalem conducted by Nahman Avigad, 1969–1982*, Vol. I: *Architecture and Stratigraphy: Areas A, W and X-2, FINAL REPORT* (Jerusalem).

Hamblin, W. J. (2007). *Solomon's Temple: Myth and History* (London).

Haran, M. (1985). *Temples and Temple Service in Ancient Israel* (Winona Lake, Indiana).

Kaufman, A. S. (1984–85). "The Meaning of *Har Habayit* and its Northern Gate" in: *Niv Hamidrashia* 18/19, 97–108.

Kenyon, K. M. (1974). *Digging Up Jerusalem* (London).

Kempinski, A. and R. Reich, eds. (1992). *The Architecture of Ancient Israel from the Prehistoric to the Persian Periods. In Memory of Immanuel (Munya) Dunayevsky* (Jerusalem).

Maier, J. (1989). "The Architectural History of the Temple Mount in Jerusalem in the Light of the Temple Scroll" in: G. J. Brooke, ed., *Temple Scroll Studies*, 23–62.

Mazar, B. (1975). *The Mountain of the Lord* (New York).

Mazar, B. (1992). *Biblical Israel: State and People* (Jerusalem).

Mazar, E. (2011). *Discovering the Solomonic Wall in Jerusalem* (Jerusalem).

Parry, D. W., ed. (1994). *Temples of the Ancient World: Ritual and Symbolism* (Salt Lake City).

Patrich, J. (2011). The Pre-Herodian Temple II: the Building Project of Simeon the Just on the Temple Mount, in: *Revue Biblique*, Tome 118.

Price, R. (2012). *Rose Guide to the Temple* (Torrance).

Ritmeyer, L. (1992). "Locating the Original Temple Mount" in: *Biblical Archaeology Review* 18.2, 24–45, 64–65.

Ritmeyer, L. and K. (2000). *From Sinai to Jerusalem: The Wanderings of the Holy Ark* (Jerusalem).

Ritmeyer, L. (2006). *The Quest: Revealing the Temple Mount in Jerusalem* (Jerusalem).

Ritmeyer, L. and K. (2015). *Jerusalem: The Temple Mount* (Jerusalem).

Rosenau, H. (1979). *Vision of the Temple: The Image of the Temple of Jerusalem in Judaism and Christianity* (London).

Schick, C. (1887). *Beit el Makdas, oder der alte Tempelplatz zu Jerusalem: Wie er jetzt ist* (Jerusalem).

Schiffman, L. H. (1994). *The Enigma of the Temple Scroll: Reclaiming the Dead Sea Scrolls* (Philadelphia and Jerusalem).

Schmitt. J. W. and J. C. Laney (1997). *Messiah's Coming Temple: Ezekiel's Prophetic Vision of the Future Temple* (Grand Rapids).

Shiloh, Y. (1984). *Excavations at the City of David. Qedem* 19 (Jerusalem).

Simons, J. (1952). *Jerusalem in the Old Testament* (Leiden).

Stevenson, K. R. (1996). "The Vision of Transformation: The Territorial Rhetoric of Ezekiel 40–48," Dissertation series (SBL), 154, (Atlanta).

Sulley, H. (1921). *The Temple of Ezekiel's Prophecy* (London).

Vaux, R. de (1961). *Ancient Israel: Its Life and Institutions* (tr. John McHugh, London).

Vogüé, M. de (1864). *Le temple de Jérusalem. Monographie du Haram ech-cherif, suivie d'un essai sur la topographie de la Ville Sainte* (Paris).

Warren, C. and C. R. Conder (1884). *Survey of Western Palestine: Jerusalem* (London).

Warren, C. (1884). *Plans, Elevations, Sections, etc., Showing the Results of the Excavations at Jerusalem, 1867–1870, Executed for the Committee of the Palestine Exploration Fund* (London).

Wilson, C. W., and C. Warren (1871). *The Recovery of Jerusalem: A Narrative of Exploration and Discovery in the City and Holy Land*, two vols. (London).

Wilson, C. W. (1880). "The Masonry of the Haram Wall" in: *Palestine Exploration Fund Quarterly Statement* (London).

Yadin, Y. (1977 [Hebrew]; 1983 [English]). *The Temple Scroll*, 3 vols. (Jerusalem).

Yadin, Y. (1985). *The Temple Scroll: The Hidden Law of the Dead Sea Sect* (London).